W9-BAG-883

MANET

manet

by Robert Rey

CROWN PUBLISHERS, INC. - NEW YORK

Title page: HENRI FANTIN-LATOUR
The Studio at the Batignolles
(*Manet Surrounded by His Friends*). Detail, 1870
Oil on canvas, 78⅞″ × 107³⁄₁₆″ (204 × 273.5 cm)
Musée d'Orsay, Paris

Translated from the French by:
EDWARD LUCIE SMITH

Series published under the direction of:
MADELEINE LEDIVELEC-GLOECKNER

Library of Congress Cataloging in Publication Data

Rey, Robert.
    Manet.

    (Crown art library)
    Translation of: Manet.
    1. Manet, Edouard, 1832-1883.   2. Painters — France —
Biography.   3. Painting, French.   4. Painting, Modern —
19th century — France.   I. Title.   II. Series.
ND553.M3R413   1988   759.4   88-7080
ISBN 0-517-03722-X

PRINTED IN ITALY – INDUSTRIE GRAFICHE CATTANEO S.P.A., BERGAMO
© 1986 BONFINI PRESS CORPORATION, NAEFELS, SWITZERLAND
NEW REVISED EDITION
ALL RIGHTS RESERVED. NO PART OF THIS BOOK MAY BE REPRODUCED OR UTILIZED IN ANY FORM OR
BY ANY MEANS, ELECTRONIC OR MECHANICAL, INCLUDING PHOTOCOPYING,
RECORDING, OR BY ANY INFORMATION STORAGE AND RETRIEVAL SYSTEM, WITHOUT
PERMISSION IN WRITING FROM THE PUBLISHER
ALL RIGHTS IN THE U.S.A. ARE RESERVED BY CROWN PUBLISHERS, INC., NEW YORK, NEW YORK

MUSIC IN THE TUILERIES, 1862
Oil on canvas, 29⅞" × 46½" (76 × 118 cm)
The National Gallery, London

Toward the middle of the nineteenth century, Courbet claimed to have replaced so-called "classic" academic art, and the fervent imaginative flights of Romanticism, by "Realism." In fact, his originality lay, not in his technique nor in his way of looking at the world, but quite simply in the themes he selected. He thus irritated his audience without surprising it. Manet, on the other hand, showed the true image of modern

Study for Music in the Tuileries, 1862
Ink wash
Private collection

existence, and this image shocked. He set himself the task of painting people, places, and things, not as people were accustomed to seeing them depicted, but exactly as he himself saw them. From the moment he felt sure of his own maturity, he did not put his knowledge of past techniques and compositions between his own vision and nature. From this sprang his rapidity of execution and his bold contrasts of harsh highlights and deep shadows. His pictures created a scandal and he challenged all the existing ideas about what was then called painting. While his career unfolded, enormous changes took place in the social and political ideas which had until then been accepted. A new era began, and Manet's paintings seemed to echo it. However, it was only by chance that he painted themes which seemed contemporary. If, as sometimes occurred, contemporary events put before him some immediate and exciting idea, he made use of this as a reporter might. But it happened only rarely. As far as we know, Manet never (except during the Franco-Prussian war of 1870) made allusion, either in his letters nor in conversation, to the very considerable events which were

6

Three Studies of a Monk Sitting
Charcoal on blue paper
Private collection

then agitating the Governments and Chancelleries of Europe.

In 1859, while he was wholly given up to painting his *Absinthe Drinker* (see page 9) war was being waged by the joint forces of France and Italy; and Italy, through skilled diplomacy, as well as through her own heroic tenacity, was making great strides toward independence. In 1861, a terrible civil war broke out in North America. It revealed to the world the

power and the tremendous wealth of the United States. In 1865, the year when the Confederate General Lee brought the war to an end by his surrender, Manet's famous *Olympia* (see pages 14-15) was shown in the Salon. A year earlier, Prussia had launched her armies against Denmark, thus heralding her hegemony over Germany. This was followed soon enough, in 1866, by the Prussian victory over Austria at Sadowa (prelude to the war of 1870 against France, which in turn was responsible for the creation of the German Emperor, who would hold sway over that newborn giant — a united Germany). And, in the year of Sadowa, Manet exhibited *The Fifer* (see page 17). Communications between countries were constantly improving. Distant nations were suddenly in the news. For example, the war which had so unwisely been started between France and Mexico ended in 1867 with a drama which shook the whole of Europe: The execution at Queretaro of the Emperor Maximilian. It was then that Manet began a picture showing the concluding act of this stupid adventure (see page 28). Industrial development took on tremendous proportions and France was covered by a network of railways. The neighborhood of the Gare St. Lazare became an artists' colony. The noisy trains, their smoke, the sparkle as they moved at top speed along the track, offered sights of an attraction as yet unexplored. Electricity began to give night a different aspect. The material progress of the world outdistanced the minds of men, who found it difficult to adjust to these changes. It is true, of course, that the trends which we now call "progressive" made their appearance well before 1848. However, the realities of proletarian existence, the sudden rise and fall of social classes, had never been shown in French literature until Emile Zola did it in his novels. Traditional, conformist morality could no longer restrain the hypersensibility of a Charles Baudelaire, who excited a whole generation by speaking to it in tones which were wholly new.

Did Manet see himself as both the end-product and the hero of this modern world the unfolding of which prefigured the future? It is easier to believe that, borne forward by the forces inherent in his time, he became its expression without even knowing it. Purely by instinct, he made the public listen to the voice, or rather to the cries, of a world in the process of giving birth to a new sort of human condition. It is thus that he takes his place, not just in the history of art, but in history. Edouard Manet's disconcerting originality lies less in what is added than in what is neglected. His paintings are perhaps both the last product and the swan-song of a social class brought to perfection and thus to extinction.

His parents, his family, were the representatives of an excellent upper-middle-class, marvels of foresight and correctness. Almost nothing linked them to the rest of the social structure. The real aristocracy meant nothing to them — they knew its

THE ABSINTHE DRINKER, 1858-1859. Oil on canvas, 69⅞″ × 40⁹⁄₁₆″ (177.5 × 103 cm)
Ny Carlsberg Glyptotek, Copenhagen

THE STREET SINGER, ca 1862
Oil on canvas
◁ 69″ × 42¾″
(175.2 × 108.6 cm)
Museum of Fine Arts, Boston

PORTRAIT OF VICTORINE MEURENT, 1862
Oil on canvas, 17″ × 17″ (43 × 43 cm)
Museum of Fine Arts, Boston
Gift of Richard C. Paine
In memory of Richard Treat Paine

11

THE ARTIST'S PARENTS, 1860.   Oil on canvas, 43⅞″ × 35¹³⁄₁₆″ (111.5 × 91 cm)
Musée d'Orsay, Paris

wretchedness and the hollowness of its pretensions. As for the commercial, or literary, or administrative bourgeoisie (the latter the concern of Balzac in his books from "Ursule Mirouet" to "Functionaries," going by way of "A Great Provincial in Paris") — it seemed ridiculous because of its naiveties and its awful lapses of taste. The urban or peasant proletariat, as spoken of by Charles Fourier or Pierre Joseph Proudhon, struck them simply by its unrealiability and lack of culture. The new industrial and managerial tycoons impressed them by their presumption, while they knew that their rise to power had often had unsavory beginnings.

M. Auguste Manet, the Artist's Father
ca 1860. Red chalk
Private collection

They no longer had appetites, merely principles: principles of justice, of honor, of conscience. True, they did not parade them; and, like the "gentlemen" of the classic period, they prided themselves on nothing. They did not even make concessions to pride of knowledge, thinking, like Pascal, that too much and too little learning were equally harmful. Each day cut them off a little more. Every other social category felt the distance from this upper-middle-class and its closed ranks.

And here we find this remoteness suddenly expressed in art. How could the public remain indifferent to this rejection? It believed that it was insulted. And so it was. It is not the technique, nor the formal aspect of a work of art which affects the spectator intimately; it is the painter's attitude toward the audience which comes across through the work. And the audience finds anything preferable to the humiliating indifference of a Manet — even provocation, which is, in itself, a kind of tribute.

Edouard Manet was born in Paris, at 5 Rue des Petits-Augustins (renamed Rue Bonaparte in 1852), on January 23, 1832. His father was chief of staff at the Ministry of Justice. His mother, *née* Fournier, was the daughter of a diplomatic emissary whose career had been spent mostly in Sweden. Maréchal Bernadotte was her godfather. Besides

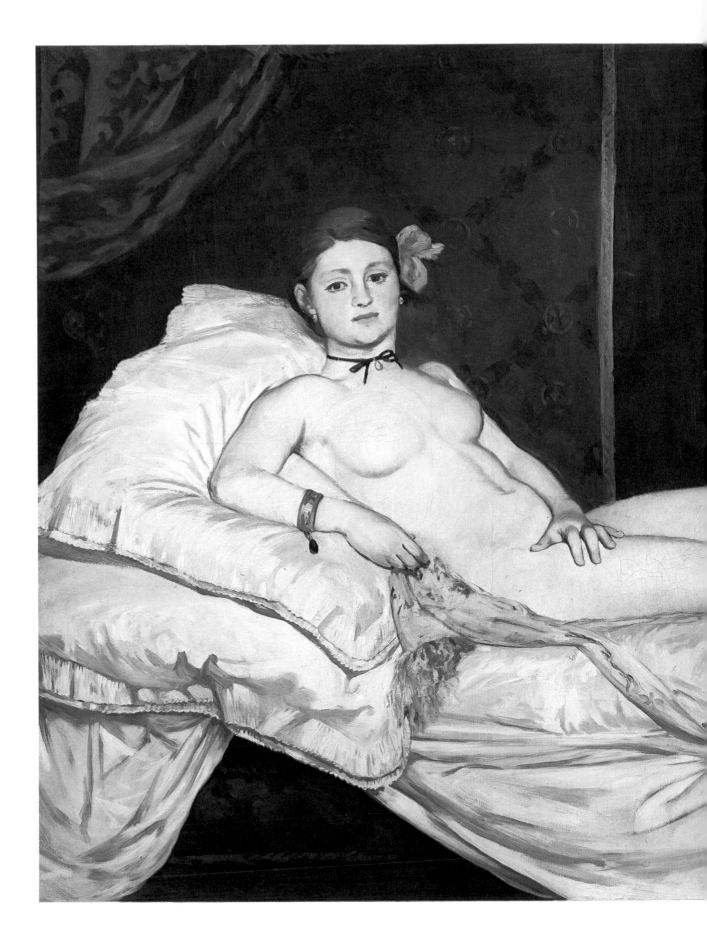

OLYMPIA, 1863
Oil on canvas
51⅜″ × 74¹³⁄₁₆″
(130.5 × 190 cm)
Musée d'Orsay
Paris

Boy with Cherries, 1858-1859.   Oil on canvas, 25%₁₆″ × 21⅝″ (65 × 55 cm)
Museu Fondaçao Calouste Gulbenkian, Lisbon

THE FIFER, 1866. Oil on canvas, 63″ × 38⁹⁄₁₆″ (160 × 98 cm)
Musée d'Orsay, Paris

Lola de Valence V/VI, 1863
Etching and aquatint, 9¼" × 6⁵⁄₁₆" (23.5 × 16.1 cm)
Bibliothèque Nationale, Paris

Edouard Manet, there were two younger sons of the marriage. We know what these parents looked like (see page 12).

Twenty-nine years had passed when their son, now become the greatest notoriety of the century, painted their portrait. The father is seated by a table; he is wearing a frock-coat and a low-crowned hat. The lower part of his face is framed in a gray beard; his expression is calm, almost severe. A little behind him stands his wife, her hair arranged in the English style, with a parting which barely shows beneath her mauve-ribboned bonnet. She is carrying a work-basket full of yarn of various strongly contrasted colors. The effect is austere, and gives a feeling of silent reflectiveness, of a penumbra wherein some bright areas are to be found, some warm tones, which become faces and outline the bodies.

Manet, who was then twenty-eight, showed this picture in the Salon of 1861. His parents no longer lived in the Rue Bonaparte — they were now at 69 Rue de Clichy, and it was there that Manet began the picture. He finished it in the studio he had just rented in the Rue de Douai. Soon after, he made an etching of the composition, and yet another in the following year, 1862.

The whole picture is filled with a secret, impassioned respect, an inner nobility, which makes us think, despite vast differences in subject and technique, of the *Peasants' Repast* by Louis Le Nain. But Manet's feelings are so intimate that the spectators of the time, excluded from any active participation and unable to accept this, tried to break into the emotional circuit by force. Léon Lagrange, the critic of the "Moniteur Universel" well expressed their displeasure: "M. and Mme M... must often have cursed the day which put a brush in the hands of this heartless portraitist."

The Spanish Singer (The Guitarero) V/V, 1861-1862. Etching, 11⅞″ × 9¾″ (30.2 × 24.7 cm)
Bibliothèque Nationale, Paris

The Dead Toreador, 1864
Etching, 6⅛″ × 8⅞″ (15.5 × 22.3 cm)

THE DEAD MAN (THE DEAD TOREADOR), 1864-1865
Oil on canvas, 29⅞″ × 60⅜″ (76 × 153.3 cm)
National Gallery of Art, Washington, D.C.

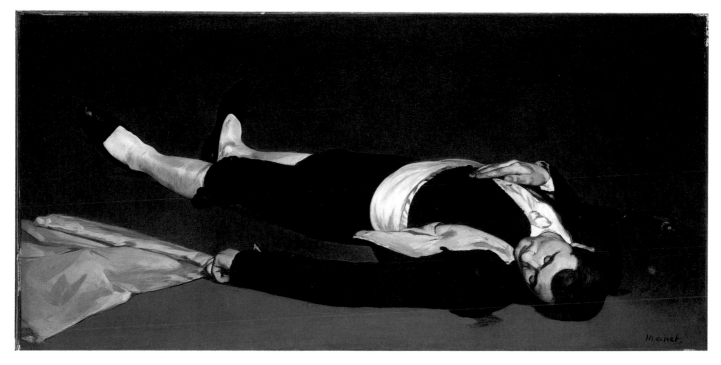

Boy with a Sword, III/III, 1862
Etching and aquatint, 10⅜″ × 6⅞″ (26.4 × 17.4 cm)
Bibliothèque Nationale, Paris

Boy with a Sword, III/IV, 1862
Etching and aquatint, 10½″ × 7¹¹/₁₆″ (26.8 × 17.9 cm)
The New York Public Library

In 1840, the young Edouard Manet, then aged seven, was sent as a day student to a school in Vaugirard (now the fifteenth *arrondissement* of Paris), where he remained for three years. At ten, he went to the Collège de la Rue des Postes (as the Collège Rollin was then called). He was an idle pupil. His great confidant was his uncle Fournier, an artillery officer. This uncle always carried his sketchbook with him, and he drew constantly. He was thus following an ancient tradition among talented artillery officers: Drawing with a view to taking the bearings of a land, of a siege, or the positions of the

21

THE PICNIC, 1863
Oil on canvas
79 1/16″ × 104 1/8″ (208 × 264.5 cm)
Musée d'Orsay, Paris

23

enemy, played an important part in military education; one could make a long and interesting list of the officers who thus occupied themselves, and of the taste they acquired for the work, from the end of the seventeenth century onward. Fournier influenced his nephew. He gave him an album of lithographs entitled *Sketches by Charlet*,[1] and the child scrawled as he pleased in the margins. The school offered a drawing class. The boy enrolled in it, despite his father's protests. There he found an accomplice, a schoolboy like himself — one Antonin Proust, who was to have a great administrative career. Thus there were three conspirators, including the Fournier uncle, who took them on Sundays to museums. Soon study was so neglected in favor of drawing that the principal of the school, M. de Faucompret alerted Manet's father.

The usual conflict between experience and vocation then began. Sentence was given: Edouard Manet was to abandon these chimeras and study law. He refused. He was offered a choice: law or the Navy. He chose the Navy and sat the entrance examination for the Ecole Navale — and failed. He was now over the age limit. Admission to the Ecole Navale was closed to him — that is unless he acquired some experience at sea before sitting the examination again. On December 9, 1848, the transport "Havre de Guadeloupe," Captain Besson, sailed for Rio. Aboard was the young Edouard Manet, now aged sixteen, entered in the ship's roll as pilot's apprentice. He returned seven months later. Another entrance examination, another failure, this time final. His father had had time to think. He had the sense to give in. At the beginning of 1850, Edouard Manet, who had just turned eighteen, entered the studio of Thomas Couture, where he was joined by his crony, Antonin Proust.

This was the beginning of a period of six years, during which the different elements of his nervous, fragile genius had time to develop. An adolescent of eighteen

Young Boy II/II, 1868-1874
Lithograph, 11⅜" × 8¹⁵⁄₁₆" (28.9 × 22.8 cm)
Bibliothèque Nationale, Paris

(1) Nicolas Charlet (1792-1845) was raised in the cult of Bonaparte and studied with Baron Gros. He specialized in history painting and produced numerous prints depicting soldiers of the French Imperial Army.

24

Young Lady in 1866 (Woman with Parrot), 1866.   Oil on canvas, 72⅞″ × 50⅝″ (185.1 × 128.5 cm)
The Metropolitan Museum of Art, New York. Gift of Erwin Davis

THE LUNCHEON
(THE LUNCHEON IN THE STUDIO), 1868
Oil on canvas, 46½″ × 60¼″ (118 × 153 cm)
Bayerische Staatsgemäldesammlungen
Neue Pinakothek, Munich

THE EXECUTION OF THE EMPEROR MAXIMILIAN, 1867-1868.   Oil on canvas, 79⁹⁄₁₆″ × 102¹⁄₁₆″ (252 × 305 cm)
Städtische Kunsthalle, Mannheim

entered Couture's studio. A man of twenty-four left it in 1856, slamming the door. If one wanted to write a novel based on his life, one would have to call it "Manet or Intelligence." Manet possessed to an exaggerated extent a sense of ridicule and of what was in bad taste. Right away he must have known the mistake he had made in going to Couture, that wonderfully clever and gifted dauber, at once cunning and naive, and prodigiously in love with himself. Yes, a dauber, the overblown flower of that race of daubers which was one of the plagues of the nineteenth century, and whose sham turbulence hid an old-fashioned respect for honors and prizes. Couture borrowed everywhere. His incontestable virtuosity, his horse-trader's instinct, served him well. He had taken a little from each of the geniuses of this time. This excellent workman watered the wine of others, diluted it, added a spice of conservative morality, and intoxicated with this poor liquor one of the most narrow-minded publics in history.

In Couture's studio Manet kept his distance. On his lips was a smile of such fine and cutting irony that the less talented soon felt his ascendency. Couture knew well enough that he had brought a dangerous thoroughbred into his fold of sheep in wolf's clothing. The master's dislike for his pupil (and it was reciprocal), was at first kept quiet, but it began on the very first day. Manet came for the models, for the tricks of the trade, and not for the aesthetic doctrine. When the studio closed, in the evening, he went to the Académie Suisse to continue working. Every week he spent long hours in the Louvre. He passionately wished to master the grammar of the arts and of draftsmanship. But he suffered a fatal disability — excessive intelligence. He "understood" too swiftly and too deeply the artist's intention in any work, so that he had no need to analyse its technique for long in order to perceive its inner life. It was those who were as quick as himself that attracted him.

He filled his notebooks with many sketches. Witness to this is the *Virgin with the White Rabbit*, which he signed M after T (Manet after Titian) and which once belonged to Denis Cochin; witness too is his interpretation of *Jupiter and Antiope*, again after Titian, and of the *Little Cavaliers*, for long attributed to Velázquez, of which he made not only a copy in oils, but also a copy in

The Execution of Maximilian, 1868
Lithograph, 13⅛" × 17" (33.3 × 43.3 cm)
The New York Public Library

The Convalescent.   Red chalk.   Musée du Louvre, Cabinet des Dessins, Paris

watercolor.   He obtained from Delacroix permission to make studies after the *Bark of Dante* (then in the Luxembourg Museum in Paris) and twice made use of this.

By the time he was twenty he was already burdened with grave cares.   Around 1848, a young Dutchwoman, Suzanne Leenhoff, two years his senior and a piano teacher, had become friendly with the Manet family.   The secret love between Suzanne Leenhoff and Edouard Manet had for consequence the birth of a child, a boy, on January 29, 1852.   His birth was registered under a borrowed name: Léon-Edouard Koëlla. Everyone around Manet accepted the boy, or pretended to accept him, as an infant brother of Suzanne Leenhoff.

Woman at Her Toilet, 1861.   Red chalk.   Courtauld Institute Galleries, London

The Cats' Rendezvous II/II, 1868.   Lithograph, 17⅛″ × 13″ (43.5 × 33.2 cm)
Bibliothèque Nationale, Paris

Often, with the help of money from his parents, Manet went traveling. He visited Holland, Germany, and Italy. He went as far as Prague and Vienna. At Florence, he painted the head of a young man, after Filippino Lippi, and made a copy of the *Venus of Urbino*, after Titian. And these were not, far from it, the only studies he made in the museums. From each of his voyages, the young man returned yet more firmly settled in his contempt for academic effects, in his wish to observe life without making it pose for him. Whence the frequent ill-humor of Couture: "You will never be anything more than the Daumier of painting." And whence, consequently, in the spring of 1856, his departure from the studio. He had learned there more good and more ill than he himself knew. Manet was then twenty-four. He made a caricature-portrait of himself around this thime. His hair is abundant. His blond beard, thick and fairly short, frames his chin and covers part of his cheeks. His neck is encircled by a gray cravat; his waistcoat is gray and his coat black. Perhaps Manet did this caricature, which is signed "a friend — Ed. Manet," for Antonin Proust, who was for long its owner.

Together with Albert de Balleroy, a painter of sporting subjects, he rented a studio. It may have been during these first days of complete freedom that he painted the bust-length *Christ with the Reed*, dated 1856. The first owner of this painting was Abbé Hurel, a childhood friend of Manet. Within a few months the studio in the Rue Lavoisier had become a meeting place for young, nonconformist painters. It was there, between the spring of 1856 and the Salon of 1859, that Manet began for the first time to try to reach a wider audience. He accumulated studies and sketches — the *Boy with Cherries* (see page 16), the model for which, a poor hypochrondiac child, was found one morning hanged in the studio (it was he who had previously posed for the *Boy with the Red Cap*); the *Child with a Sheep*, which shows, in a landscape setting, a little naked shepherd-boy clasping a lamb in his arms; the *Woman with Dogs*; the *Woman with a Jar*; and the *Portrait of Abbé Hurel*. There, too, he did the *Absinthe Drinker*. This work, which was to be flaty rejected by the jury of the Salon of 1869, was the fruit of long meditation.

Manet had not broken off all relations with Couture, but their meetings were lacking in cordiality. In painting his *Absinthe Drinker*, Manet calculated on upsetting his old teacher. His model was a derelict called Collardet, whose habitual drunkeness still had something of the grand manner about it. He showed him leaning against a wall skirted by a narrow bench. On this the drunkard has put down his glass, half-full of opal-colored poison. The bottle, a bullet-shaped object with a long neck, has rolled to the ground. The man is draped in a romantic cape; a large tall-crowned hat, very high and spreading, covers him almost to the level of the eyes. The face, seen between this hat which

THE HARBOR AT CALAIS, 1871
Oil on canvas
32⅛″ × 39⅝″ (81.5 × 100.7 cm)
Private collection, Switzerland

On the Beach, 1873
Oil on canvas
23½″ × 28¹³⁄₁₆″ (59.6 × 73.2 cm)
Musée d'Orsay, Paris

almost swallows it from above, and the beard which covers the cheeks below, is at once brutish and soft. It is lit from one side only. The cloak does not cover the body from the knees down. The man is propped on his right leg, while the left, stretched in front of him, touching the ground with its point, seems to sketch out involuntarily the steps of a dance (see page 9). Indeed, there was much that was new in this use of thick paint, contained within brush-contours made in brown, and in these glistening soot-blacks. It was evident then — and would for long be evident — where Manet took these effects: It was Couture himself who pursued this highly contrasted modelling of the faces, these sharp, dark shadows. But Manet did not use them with coquetry, like his teacher; he pushed them to their limits, thus obtaining effects of tragic intensity — like Daumier, in fact. Couture had not been so far off in his prophecy — if he had restrained himself from that "anything more than" and from bitterness, he would have proved accurate.

Couture, when invited to see the picture at the Rue Lavoisier, before it was sent off to the Salon, let it be seen that he thought it the work of insanity, and treated the painter as if he himself were the "drunkard." The break was final. A few days later the jury of the Salon rejected Manet's entry, as might have been expected. After this first skirmish with the Salon, Manet's name began to go around the studios. Sometimes he was regarded as a victim, sometimes as a madman. At the same time the Galerie Martinet opened on the Boulevard des Italiens, and brought the man in the street face to face with these works in which a new feeling was manifest. The era of scandal began.

The *Absinthe Drinker* has a certain clumsiness, or rather a somewhat shrivelled stiffness. Manet showed greater freedom in another picture, much more original, which was painted in 1860: the *Music in the Tuileries* (see page 5). The whole picture is the result of free observation. Its components — trees, foliage, figures — are painted as colored volumes that are imbued with their own tints, but are also of color and form by virtue of the fact that they are in motion, either absolutely or in a relative sense. No picture, throughout the whole length of the nineteenth century, depicts so well the dynamism of nature. It is only rivaled in this by some sketches painted by Jean-Baptiste Carpeaux. Certainly in no other picture is the enhancement of some colors by shadow so clearly brought out, and none recreates on canvas the fugitive yet total vision of a single moment in such unique fashion, without literary or intellectual prolongations.

It is known that Albert de Balleroy provided one silhouette for the picture, and that another silhouette evokes Manet himself. Others "appear" in the picture — the writer, critic, and sculptor Zacharie Astruc, and Mme Lejosne (whose officer husband was a friend of Baudelaire's). Gioacchino Rossini, Jacques Offenbach, Baudelaire, the writer

THE BALCONY, 1868-1869.   Oil on canvas, 66½″ × 49¼″ (169 × 125 cm)
Musée d'Orsay, Paris

◁

REPOSE:
PORTRAIT OF BERTHE MORISOT, 1870
Oil on canvas, 58¼″ × 43¾″ (147.8 × 111 cm)
Museum of Art
Rhode Island School of Design, Providence

IN THE GARDEN, 1870
Oil on canvas
17½″ × 21¼″ (44.5 × 54 cm)
The Shelburne Museum
Shelburne, Vermont

◁

PORTRAIT OF EMILE ZOLA, 1868
Oil on canvas
57⅝″ × 44⅞″ (146.3 × 114 cm)
Musée d'Orsay, Paris

READING, 1865-1873
Oil on canvas
23¹³⁄₁₆″ × 28¹⁵⁄₁₆″ (60.5 × 73.5 cm)
Musée d'Orsay, Paris

41

Study of Woman. Ink wash
Neue Pinakothek, Munich

Théophile Gautier and Champfleury, the journalist Aurélien Scholl, and the painters Charles Monginot and Henri Fantin-Latour. Did they all sit for it? Evidently not. Did they sit at all, in fact? Manet gave his figures shapes which he drew from memory. He made use of them. There is no likeness between a work of this kind and the "réunions" which Fantin-Latour was already planning at this period; but there are many links, for example, with the *Moulin de la Galette*, painted fifteen years later, for which Auguste Renoir made use of his friends with no thought of handing down to the future the particular details of their appearances. For three years the picture remained in the studio. At the same time Manet had undertaken the portrait of his father and mother. And as he was making etchings and watercolors — he often took up and reused old motifs in one or another of these mediums.

One of the last pictures done in 1860 was the *Spanish Singer* (see engraving page 19): First fruits of the taste for things Spanish which had taken hold of Manet, more or less at the time when the guitarist Huerta (composer of the "Hymn to Riego") became the rage of Paris. The singer is seated on a bench, with his instrument resting in his lap. A pink scarf is wound around his head, under a black hat with a flat brim, and contrasts strangely with a brick-red and brown background in the manner of Van Dyck. The visit to Paris of a group of singers and dancers had awakened in Manet an ardent curiosity about types and costumes whose colors seemed those he had been waiting for. This time the jury of the Salon favored him: Not only was the *Spanish Singer* accepted, it even received an honorable mention. Théophile Gautier, in his "Abécédaire du Salon de 1861," gave a truculent description of it. Gautier found there material for literature. He asked no more of a painting. In any case, his sensibility to the visual arts was more or less nil. Jean-Baptiste Corot and Jean-François Millet already knew something of this. Manet would soon learn it.

It was at this time that Manet, leaving the Rue de Douai, took a new studio in the Rue Guyot. He was to live there until 1871. His ardor for things Spanish did not, however, prevent him from painting scenes in the area surrounding Paris, such as the picture called *Fishing* (Metropolitan Museum of Art, New York), featuring Suzanne Leenhoff (soon to become Mme Manet) and the little Köella. But he did return constantly to Spanish themes. He went so far as to reuse the *Little Cavaliers*, this time in order to paint a sort of studio scene at the time of Philipp IV. The picture shows Velázquez at work, surrounded by noblemen. Yet another picture shows the same noblemen being brought fruit on a platter by a little boy (Léon Köella). When he interrupted his work on these evocations, it was in order to make studies of the nude — for these Suzanne Leenhoff served as model. But Spain soon called to him again — in a second study of the young Köella. The child is shown carrying a heavy sword in both arms — the sheath knocks against his legs (Metropolitan Museum of Art, New York). Manet made two etchings from the painting (see page 21).

*Studies of Women. Ink wash
Neue Pinakothek, Munich*

Carried away by his taste for the picaresque, Manet assembled, in a frieze-like composition nearly three yards in length, not only his absinthe drinker, but an old Jew, a wandering musician and beggar, who was celled Guéroult, a turbanned Saracen, two little boys, and a little gypsy carrying a baby. This strange work, known under the title of *The Old Musician* (National Gallery, Washington, D.C.), is not without a relationship, both through its mystery and its elements of the incongruous, with the well-known *Studio* by Courbet. And to the *Old Musician*, Manet soon painted a charming pendant: the *Street Singer* (see

THE LEMON, 1880-1881
Oil on canvas
5½″ × 8⅝″ (14 × 22 cm)
Musée d'Orsay, Paris

44

page 10). This time the model was a young woman called Victorine Meurent, who played the violin and also modelled. In a dozen years she posed many times for Manet. In works like the *Boy with Sword*, and the *Street Singer*, Manet confirmed an already apparent taste for faces which seemed like those of somnambulists. They gaze unseeingly, and follow an unknown dream behind the clear yet impenetrably dark crystal of their eyes. This way of staring down the audience without even seeming to be aware of it counted, at that time, as a crowning insolence: Manet was rarely without it. But we cannot go on for long without again talking of Spain. This time a picture of a *Gypsy with Cigarette* (The Art Museum, Princeton University, New Jersey); then, for an overdoor, a guitar and a sombrero; then again a group of Spanish dancers, one of them seated — this is the first appearence of *Lola de Valence*. The models formed part of a troupe led by the dancer Mariano Campruni which was having a success at the Hippodrome. Almost as soon as he had done the group, Manet began the full-length portrait, half life-size, of *Lola* (see engraving page 18). Baudelaire wrote a well-known quatrain about this dancer, her bust draped in a black mantilla, wearing a full-skirted dress with tassels. The poet compared her to a black and rose-colored jewel. It is also well known that certain misguided critics called him immoral for writing the poem. The picture is among the most celebrated by Manet. But is it among his best? Not at all. Genius can make certain demands — Manet's is certainly entitled to make them. But *Lola de Valence* is a summary of all his weaknesses. The face is sketched in thick brown outlines — these do not convey any feeling of relief or depth. The right arm lacks solidity, the left leg is sunk in shadow; the dancer rests on a foot which is completely lifeless. The pompons of red wool which adorn her dress look like flat dots. All the tricks with dark paints which Manet had learned in Couture's studio come out again here. And unfortunately, there was yet more of it left to come. The few well-painted details — such as the right leg in its stocking of coarse silk — put the picture out of balance rather than helping it. It is both astonishing and irritating to find that Manet could be contented with so little. It reveals the "amateur" side of his talent, and his tendency to stop halfway. For this reason, the picture shows how very dangerous Manet could be as an influence. However, apart from Jean-Baptiste Chardin and Paul Cézanne, one can find very few masters whose entire *œuvre* is exemplary. Besides this, *Lola* has had a certain amount of bad luck. In the Camondo Collection in the Louvre, the picture was for long hung next to two implacable touchstones: *The Model in the Studio*, by Courbet, and Cézanne's little sketch, *The Cardplayers*. It did not stand up well to the comparison.

In 1862 Manet also painted a portrait of his younger brother Eugène "dressed as a Majo," one of Victorine Meurent "in the Costume of an Espada" (both at the

Head of a Woman
Red chalk
Bibliothèque Nationale, Paris

Metropolitan Museum of Art, New York), and one of a woman reclining. The sitter was Jeanne Duval, Baudelaire's mistress, and the picture is now in the Budapest Museum. It shows her seated, gaunt and brown-skinned, wearing a huge crinoline. Baudelaire brought her to Manet's studio during the summer of 1862. Manet did the portrait in a single sitting. He also painted several portraits of friends, some still lifes, and watercolors.

And in progress was the *Picnic* (see pages 22-23). We are approaching the famous year 1863, during which, on a wave of indignation, the name of Edouard Manet was to spread throughout the world of art. Manet had been preparing the picture since the summer of 1862. He made studies for the landscape background, near Gennevilliers. The models were Victorine Meurent, Eugène Manet, and the Dutch sculptor Ferdinand Leenhoff, Suzanne Leenhoff's brother. In secret, Manet put together his composition on lines taken from Raphael: the *Judgment of Paris*. He finished the work, dated it 1863, and submitted it to the jury of the Salon, together with the

Study of Nude, Sitting
Black ink and chalk on blue-gray paper
Private collection

46

Study for Woman at Her Toilet
Red chalk on paper used for printer's proof
Private collection

After the Bath, 1860-1861
Red chalk, 11″ × 7⅞″ (28 × 20 cm)
The Art Institute, Chicago

Young Man in the Costume of a Majo and the *Portrait of Victorine Meurent in the Costume of an Espada.* All three were rejected. However, the exclusions were so numerous that the protests of the victims reached Napoleon III. This provided the Emperor with the pretext for one of those nonconformist gestures, of which there were several examples in his curious career, and which help to make him a likeable personality. The whole thing amounted to a revolution. The Emperor himself wished to see the rejected works, to touch them with his own hand. By his express command the ill-will of officialdom and the obstacles which it raised up were overtuned: The "Salon des Réfusés" was opened in the Palais de l'Industrie, right beside the official Salon — in fact, one exhibition led straight into the other. The Emperor, and the Empress with him, went to visit it. It included, besides pictures by Manet, works by James McNeill Whistler, Johan Barthold Jongkind, Henri Fantin-Latour, Camille Pissarro, Jean-Charles Cazin, the engraver Félix Bracquemond, and the sculptor Henri Cros. Also on view were canvasses signed J. P. Laurens, Henri Harpignies, Antoine Chintreuil, Pierre Legros, and Antoine Vollon. The public was academic by instinct. It went to hoot. However some writers rushed to the defense: Fernand Desnoyers, Théophile Thoré (Thoré-Bürger), Edouard Lockroy, and, above all, Emile Zola, who praised Manet for having realized the dream of every painter — that of placing natural figures in a real landscape. He made much of this "huge ensemble, full of air..." The vulgar, with their liking for formulas, chattered of "pleinairisme." This was, of course, a misinterpretation.

The *Picnic* is not a picture painted on the spot, like some of Corot's sketches. Instead, it is a picture painted in the studio, like the *Concert* by Giorgione. Even its technique is not unprecedented. Why, then, was it such a shock to people's eyes and to their preconceptions? Simply because those areas in full light, and those in shadow, instead of passing very gradually one into the other, were sharply contrasted; hence the picture's crude, harsh look, the stereotyped way in which one form is imposed on another. Courbet, by his habit of modelling very much in the round — "it's always three billiard balls" said Manet — kept natural appearances at arm's length, and remained on the whole faithful to the practice of treating painting as if it were sculpture, accentuating plasticity to an exaggerated extent. Courbet took this from the school of David, to which he was directly linked through his early teachers. On the other hand, Manet, treating the face and body with a modelling which was barely perceptible, rediscovered the intense realism which is to be seen in some of Holbein's portraits. But Holbein was so long forgotten that to revive him was the equivalent of committing an intolerable novelty. The uproar was at its height among both crities and artists when Manet embarked upon that supreme masterpiece, his *Olympia*. This showed Victorine Meurent, lying on a bed, wearing a pearl and a gold bracelet. Her left hand rests on the upper part of her right thigh — a gesture to be seen again in the nymph who lies in the foreground of Poussin's *Triumph of Flora* in the Louvre. In the background is a negress in a bandanna carrying a bouquet. At the foot of the bed, a black cat arches its back (see pages 14-15). Here, too, Manet could cite precedents — in Titian and in Goya. And here, too, the difference in technique between this work and works universally tolerated was reduced to almost nothing. But this infintesimal difference was enough to reduce visitors to the Salon of 1863 almost to a state of madness. The weaknesses of *Lola de Valence* are not to be found in *Olympia*. The colors which were there lacking

BALL AT THE OPERA, 1873
Oil on canvas, 23¼″ × 28½″ (59 × 72.5 cm)
National Gallery of Art, Washington, D.C.
Gift of Mrs. Horace Havemeyer
In memory of Louisine W. Havemeyer

49

BOATING, 1874
Oil on canvas
38½″ × 51¼″ (97.2 × 130.2 cm)
The Metropolitan Museum of Art, New York
The H.O. Havemeyer Collection

ARGENTEUIL, 1874
Oil on canvas
58¹¹⁄₁₆″ × 45¼″ (149 × 115 cm)
Musée des Beaux-Arts, Tournai, Belgium
◁

MONET PAINTING IN HIS BOAT, 1874
Oil on canvas, 32¹¹⁄₁₆″ × 39⅜″ (83 × 100 cm)
Bayerische Staatsgemäldesammlungen
Neue Pinakothek, Munich

Young Woman, Sitting
India ink
Private collection

in refinement are now of infinite delicacy. In the folds of the sheet plays a gray without parallel. Manet seems to have thrust back the shadows which mark the roundness of a volume right to the bounding contour. The shadows are all incredibly thin, done with miraculous subtlety. The form thus achieves roundness without losing any of its natural clearness. Not since Cranach's *Venus* had the image of a nude body been shown so truly naked, freed of the marks with which the pursuit of sculptural volume in painting had stained it — this after a lapse of four hundred years. Such a well-established custom was not be overthrown in a day.

Painting is a sort of code. Even children read this code easily enough, as if it came to them completely naturally, but only on condition that it conforms to ancestral practice and common usage. Because Manet's realism was expressed, so to speak, in a forgotten alphabet, the public remained aghast in front of his *Olympia*. Of course people saw, even in spite of themselves, the intense truth of this nude. They found themselves in the presence, not of some ideographic theme, but of a naked body. I remember my own first meeting — more than sixteen years ago — with *Olympia*, and the oddly painful shock which the picture gave me. I was afraid when I saw this pallid form, this small face where the skin seemed stretched over a piece of wood. *Olympia* frightened me like a corpse — yet I felt weighing upon me the evil spell cast by those eyes which were so full of life. Is it necessary to recall the storm which went up? In nearly all the criticall accounts one finds the same horror at this nudity, too truthfully exact in color. It reminded people of the bodies to be seen only in medical school. "The crowd pressed around M. Manet's corrupt *Olympia* as if it found itself in a morgue" (Paul de Saint-Victor, in the "Presse," May 28, 1865). "The flesh tones are dirty, the modelling nil" (Théophile Gautier, in the "Moniteur Universel," June 24). "This reddish brunette is of wonderful ugliness; her face is stupid, her skin cadaverous... this wild mix-up of disparate colors, of impossible forms, hits one in the eye and stuns one" (Felix Deriège, in "Le Siècle," June 2). And so on.

Manet could not foresee what a "classic" his work was to become: the subscription which would be opened, seven years after his death, to present it to the French National Collection; the hesitations of his old friend, Antonin Proust, now become Minister of Fine Arts; the final transfer of *Olympia* to the Louvre in November 1907 (forty-two years later) on the orders of Clémenceau, who thus fulfilled a prophecy made by Zola. Yet the majority of the horrified was in fact opposed by a minority of enthusiasts. Manet might have said, with Vauvenargues, that "it is no great evil not to succeed with everybody." A whole groupe of defenders supported him with passionate zeal. Zacharie Astruc, who had already greeted *Lola de Valence* with lyrical enthusiasm, Baudelaire, the astonishing M. Chocquet (who had a post at the Ministry of Finance and who collected contemporary art), Zola (who was about to begin, in the "Evénement," such a vigorous campaign in favor of Manet that indignant readers demanded that the editor, Villemessant, get rid of his critic, which he did), the liberal leader Théodore Duret, and many others. Soon their headquarters was the famous Café Guerbois, at 9 Avenue de Clichy. This was, till 1875, the meeting place of those painters and writers who were known for being uncompromising. Manet was, by his distinction, his lively wit, spiced by a trifle of dandyism, its most brilliant habitué. Despite his apparent carelessness, he worked tremendously hard. He made flower studies, racecourse scenes, portraits, and watercolors; in addition, he tackled themes drawn from the events of the day — for example the naval duel which took place off Cherbourg on June 19, 1864, between the corvette of the United States Navy *Kearsage*, and the Confederate vessel *Alabama*. However, he detested the anecdotal. He seemed to want to show that the drama of any action is a subjective phenomenom, not something spectacular. Who would think, confronted with this handful of little boats filled with tourists in top hats, all looking toward the horizon where two hulks are silhouetted in clouds of cotton-wool smoke, that this was a fight to the death?

In 1867, he made four different attemps to paint the *Execution of the Emperor Maximilian*, an event which had shaken Europe (see pages 28 and 29). But how did he tackle it? He showed only what human eyes might have taken in, in the agitation of the terrible moment when the platoon's volley rang out. He knew that during these moments everything speeded up, and that, had he happened to be there, he would have seen almost nothing of the drama: the bent backs of a few soldiers, their cheeks against the butts of their rifles; the whiteness of their belts; one guard quietly reloading his weapon; and, in front of them, seen through the smoke, three vague silhouettes. In sum, a few details fixed by the retina, and transmitted to the memory, upon which they engraved themselves. The terror of the scene was something subjective, and Manet rejected all subjectivity. He was not a storyteller. If he sometimes painted things which, as here,

THE GAME OF CROQUET, 1873
Oil on canvas, 28½″ × 41¾″ (72.5 × 106 cm)
Städelsches Kunstinstitut, Frankfurt

he had not actually seen, he showed them from an angle of bare, positive realism, and in the most prosaic manner possible.

Whether he was painting a portrait, or depicting an intensely dramatic action, Manet always took up the same attitude to the audience. He put the facts before it, but, disdainfully, refused to make a public avowal of his emotions. In 1865 he painted *Angelina* (Luxembourg Museum, Paris), the *Spanish Woman with the Black Cross*, and *Jesus Mocked by the Soldiers* (The Art Institute of Chicago). For the latter he used as model one Janvier, a locksmith by trade, thus returning to the tradition of the painters of the Middle Ages, and to that of the Spanish painters of the seventeenth century, who often found their models among humble artisans. In the same year he also painted, as Velázquez and Ribera had done, authentic down-and-outs, calling them philosophers. By the end of 1865, Manet had become truly himself.

Pascal is still right: "It is the battle which pleases us, and not the victory... We never go in search of things, but in search of the quest." Thus we may, from this time on, think of the Manet problem as being unravelled. The paintings come more rapidly. They have no further surprises to offer us. The *Woman with Parrot* (see page 25), the *Woman Playing the Guitar*, the *Matador Saluting* (Metropolitan Museum of Art, New York), and the whole series of bullfight pictures show Manet confirmed in his course, and in the free employment of his own instinctive virtuosity. It is worth noting that this marks the end of his enthusiasm for Spanish subjects. His passion for Spain had been sated during his travels there in 1865.

Manet's most important work of 1866 is *The Fifer* (see page 17). Victorine Meurent probably posed for it. The picture was built up in three stages with a sureness and quickness of hand which no other artist has ever surpassed. In Couture's studio Manet had been taught to prepare a picture in monochrome. Now he rejected such leading-strings. He painted straight on to a canvas which had been simply given a ground of unified color. Light and shade were arrived at by the most economical means. The transitions from one to the other were yet narrower and more skilfully calculated in their unbelievable suddeness than in the days when he painted the *Olympia*. To the face, and the flesh-tones, he gave a wonderfully living texture, first establishing them by means of a middle tone, then laying in the shadows, and then finally adding the highlights. He never bothered to hide his *pentimenti*, simply coverig them up with a broad brush-stroke of color through which the tone thus concealed glimmered, giving the happiest of effects. He mixed his colors very little. Seen from close-up, the red breeches seem all one tone, like a lacquer. But a few touches of black, hardly visible when one is looking at the canvas from close-up serve, as soon as one gets away from

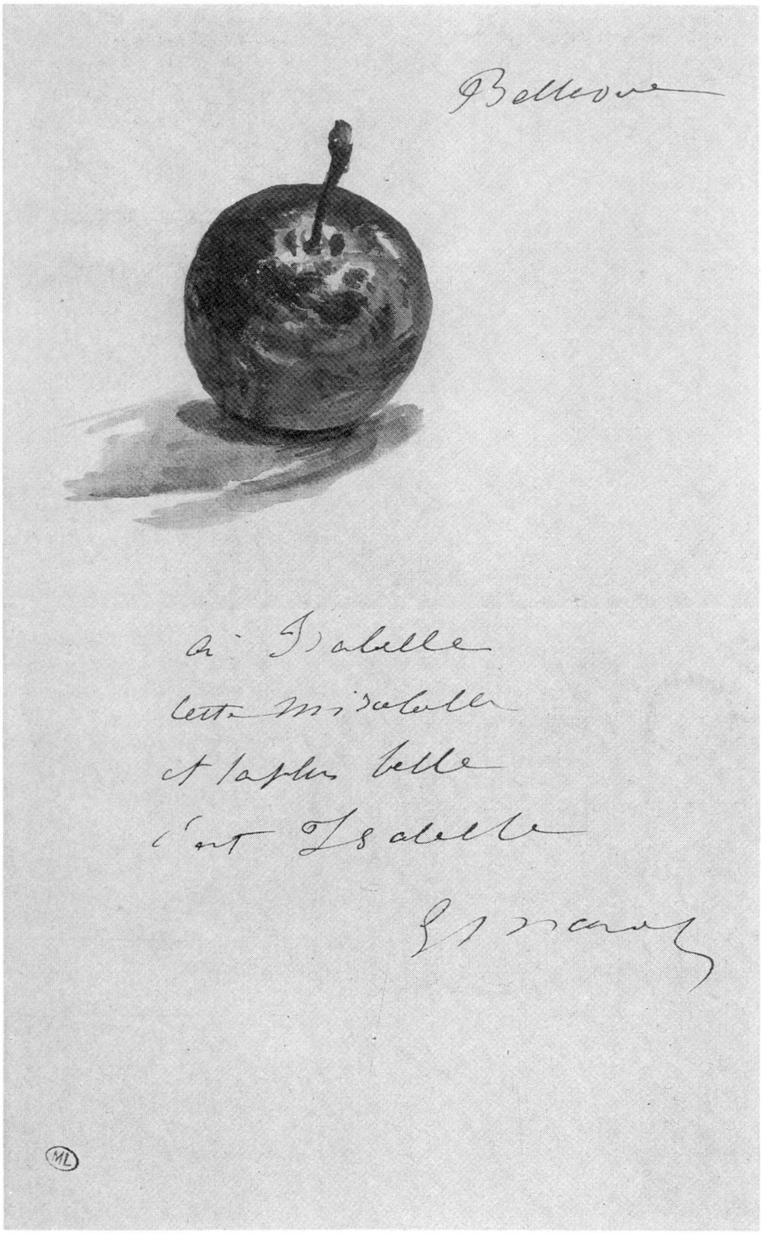

The Mirabelle Plum, 1880
Letter with watercolor to
Isabelle Lemonnier
"To Isabelle this mirabelle ..."
Musée du Louvre
Cabinet des Dessins, Paris

it, to give splendid modelling to the coarse uniform-cloth. This work, too, used to hang near to the little model by Corot, and to Cézanne's *Cardplayers*. But it held its own.

Was Manet, then, without weaknesses? Not at all. We can see how, very often, in his minor works, the intellect was too quick for the painter's hand, and spoilt the picture. Many of his flower paintings are too summary, and are lacking in refinement. The little portrait of *Mme Manet at the Piano* (Musée d'Orsay, Paris) is at the same time exquisite and deplorable. The charming silhouette of the player, seated in profile at

Isabelle with a Bonnet, 1880
Letter with watercolor to
Isabelle Lemonnier
"If you come, as I hope
it would be best if you came
on Sunday ..."
Musée du Louvre
Cabinet des Dessins, Paris

her instrument, stands out against a gray background which is far too little modulated. The moldings of the wainscot are put in with rigid strokes which are too dark, so that they seem to be in front of the model, not behind her. The wood of the piano is thickly and monotonously painted, without transparency.

In 1867 the Paris World Fair took place. Manet decided to do what Courbet had done in 1865 and was to do again on this occasion. He decided to put up a building at his own cost and to exhibit in it most of the works which we have just been discussing.

In this hall, Manet's detractors confronted his faithful admirers. He had, however, only one real defender in the press: Zola. As some return for his debt to this faithful friend, Manet painted, the year after, the portrait which is now in the Orsay Museum (see page 40). And the figure of Berthe Morisot put in an appearance, in the painting called *The Balcony* (see page 37). Her family were Manet's relations, and she was to become one of his favorite models.

During the Franco-Prussian war and the siege of Paris, Manet, who was aged thirty-nine, served as an artilleryman in the National Guard. By an ironic coincidence, his commanding officer was the genre painter Jean Meissonier. He took everything calmy. In his letters to his family, he counselled patience and tried to reassure them... "I will be at the Porte de Saint-Ouen, I shall get on very well there." (November 7, 1870)... "Take care of your health. Don't worry. Be patient. We are very patient here. I'm always thinking of you." In a letter, dated January 30, 1871, he wrote to his wife who was staying at Oloron-Sainte-Marie, near Arcachon with her husband's mother and the little Léon Koëlla: "It is all over and all three of us (Manet and his two brothers), are still alive and in one piece." At the beginning of February, he left Paris. He painted several views of the harbor at Arcachon, and then, returning to Paris, worked with his usual industriousness.

Study of a Fisherman
India ink and watercolor
Private collection

It was possible to believe, in 1873, that a reconciliation was about to take place between the public, officialdom, and Manet. He showed in the Salon *Le Bon Bock* (Philadelphia Museum of Art). The model was the engraver Bellot, shown smoking his pipe, seated facing the spectator and near to a table on which is a big glass of beer. His large stomach rests on his thighs. Unanimous praise succeeded abuse. One has to go back, perhaps, to the appearance of Ingres's *Vow of Louis XIII*, in the Salon of 1824, fo find a parallel

THE GRAND CANAL, VENICE (BLUE VENICE), 1875
Oil on canvas, 23⅛″ × 28⅛″ (58.7 × 71.4 cm)
The Shelburne Museum
Shelburne, Vermont

Horses, Carts, and Boats.   Drawing.   Private collection

reversal of opinion.   Given Manet's temperament, this popularity disturbed him.   He was quick to disenchant the public.

A marked change was about to take place in his palette.   In 1874, a whole group of painters, Claude Monet, Camille Pissarro, Paul Cézanne, Alfred Sisley, Auguste Renoir and several others held their first collective exhibition, called today that of "The Impressionists."   Most of these painters were somewhat younger than Manet (however, Pissarro, who was born in 1830, was two years older).   The tolerance of the Second Empire juries, in the period 1863 to 1870, had given several of them entry to the Salon. But, after the Paris Commune, [2] all non-academic painting was held to be "communard" and hostile to public order.   For four years these men, in spite of themselves, had had to live alone with nature.   They had rid themselves of the influences visible in their

(2) Revolutionary government created in Paris and in some provincial cities after March 18, 1871, at the end of the Franco-Prussian war.   This insurrection against the bourgeois government of Versailles was squashed during the "bloody week" of May 22-28.

early works.   They used a very high-key palette.   They showed nature in its least formal aspect, and were inspired by the example of Manet.   But, in return, they had an influence on Manet himself.   His palette lightened considerably.   The dark tones, the frequent use of shadows, which till now had been seen in his work, were to be succeeded by a new brilliancy and transparency.

The Laundry, rejected by the Salon of 1876 with only two votes in favor (those of Léon Bonnat and Jean-Jacques Henner!) was exhibited at the studio which he then occupied, at 5 Rue Saint Pétersbourg.   Invitations were sent to all the newspapers.   The result was a complete reversal and a torrent of abuse no less violent than in earlier days. Manet was not a man who made concessions.   All the time, he was creating superb pictures, like the *Portrait of Stéphane Mallarmé*, which among all his small portraits, may be considered the most successful (see page 65).   With these small pictures alternated large portraits, like that of *Nana* (see page 67) in her dressing-room, which probably suggested to Zola the title of his novel; and the portrait of Faure, the baritone, as Hamlet, and that of M. and Mme Jules Guillemet *In the Conservatory* (see page 75); and the one of *Père Lathuille* at home (Tournai Museum, Belgium).   Faced with the number of pictures of all kinds which he painted every year, one is astonished by the certainty of his art, by his incredible talent for self-renewal.   From the *At Père Lathuille's*, for

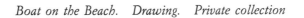

Boat on the Beach.   Drawing.   Private collection

MADAME MANET ON A BLUE SOFA, 1874
Pastel on paper mounted on canvas
19¹¹⁄₁₆″ × 24″ (50 × 61 cm)
Musée d'Orsay, Paris

64

Portrait of the Poet Stéphane Mallarmé, 1876
Oil on canvas
$10^{13}\!/_{16}'' \times 14^{1}\!/_{8}''$ (27.5 × 36 cm)
Musée d'Orsay, Paris

BEFORE THE MIRROR, 1876-1877.   Oil on canvas, 36¼″ × 28⅛″ (92.1 × 71.4 cm)
The Solomon R. Guggenheim Museum, New York. Gift of Justin K. Thannhauser

NANA, 1877. Oil on canvas, 60⅝″ × 45¼″ (154 × 115 cm)
Kunsthalle, Hamburg

WOMAN WITH THE GARTER, 1879. Pastel on canvas, 21⅝″ × 18⅛″ (55 × 46 cm)
Ordrupgaardsamlingen, Charlottenlund, Copenhagen

which all the studies were made in the open air, to the *Bar at the Folies-Bergère* (see pages 82-83), shown in the Salon of 1882, for which all the studies were made at the Folies-Bergère itself, by completely artificial lighting, his works are redolent of something so real an new as almost to confuse the viewer.

Manet's other submission to the Salon of 1882 was almost universally well received. This was *Jeanne*, or *Spring*, portrait of Jeanne de Marsy, a young actress who was to make a big career in the theater. From 1880 onward, Manet began to feel the effects of the disease which was eventually to kill him. This disease originated in overwork, in the excessive strains imposed on a being who, while wishing to appear calm and smiling, had sustained for nearly twenty years a harassing struggle against the incomprehension, the ill-will, and the frivolousness of the public he wished to conquer. It began with brief attacks of rheumatism. These became more and more frequent, and more and more painful. He was painting portraits, because these made it less necessary for him to stand upright in front of an easel. During the summer of 1880,

Loth and His Daughters. Conté crayon. Private collection

Study for Olympia, 1862-1863.   Red chalk, 8⅞″ × 11¹³⁄₁₆″ (22.5 × 30 cm)
Bibliothèque Nationale, Paris.

he went for a rest to Bellevue.   His subjects were mostly flowers, still lifes, and small landscapes, painted with a brilliancy, a transparency of tone of which one never tires. At the Salon, he was represented by a huge portrait of his childhood friend, Antonin Proust (Toledo Museum of Art, Ohio).   In 1881, though his illness was getting worse, he found the strength to execute the *Portrait of Henri Rochefort* (Kunsthalle, Hamburg), which was shown in the Salon, and the vast picture known as *Monsieur Pertuiset*, one of Manet's liveliest and most unexpected works, and also one of his most luminous (Museu de Arte, São Paulo).   Pertuiset — famous at that moment as a big-game hunter in Africa — displays, just at the very moment when the public would have liked to see him full of the emotions of the hunt, the impenetrably phlegmatic air which Manet puts, like a sheet of glass, between the spectator and the model. In painting this picture, he had the bitter joy of knowing that it had not lost him a single opponent.   Yet, it got into the Salon by a surprising number of voices.   Alexandre Cabanel, the chairman of the jury, dared to say, "Gentlemen, there is not one among us fit to do a head like that *en plein air.*" The picture got seventeen votes.

When the results were declared, on June 24, 1881, it was discovered that Manet had received a second class medal. The news was met with howlings and booings. Manet made no adherents. Even some writers who might have been expected to know better, such as J. K. Huysmans, could not accept the picture. "M. Manet took pleasure in swathing the earth in violet — an innovation of no great interest and far too facile,"[3] Huysmans wrote that year. One thing remains from all these puerile objections: Manet had come a long way from the simplified doctrine of the Couture studio. He had mastered the use of local color. He had also learned — from the Impressionists, who, in turn, owed him so much in the field of direct observation — that shadow is not only a shading of local color toward black but a decomposition of light in a particular area or on a surface, and that it can be captured and depicted only with cold tints.

(3) *L'Art moderne*, p. 182.

*Study for a Scene on a Beach (Boulogne, Arcachon, or Berck). Black pencil
Private collection*

Huysmans, and so many others with him, belonged to a class of critics for whom a painting is merely the illustration of some literary concept.

Alphonse de Neuville, an excellent painter lost in a desert of the anecdotal, soon wrote to let Manet know that henceforth he was considered worthy of official recognition, and that the next Legion of Honor would be considered "as justice done to the sincerity and the character of your talent".

The year 1881 was fruitful in portraits and other pictures. Manet spent the summer at Versailles and, on his return to Paris that autumn, immediately began work, in his studio at 77 Rue d'Amsterdam, on the *Bar at the Folies-Bergère*. It was to be his last picture of large size. In this work, Manet plays off his beautiful blacks with supreme charm against the brightness of the flowered cloth and the big mirror in which is reflected, behind the young barmaid, the bustle of the music-hall. But his illness grew worse. On January 1, 1882, Antonin Proust, Minister for the Fine Arts in the Gambetta Government, awarded Manet the star of Chevalier of the Legion of Honor.

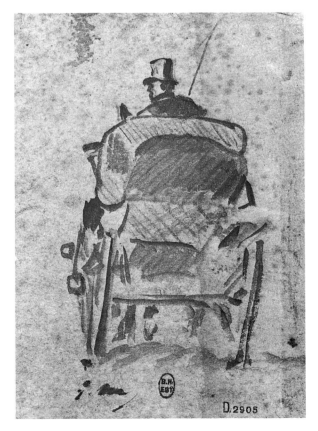

The Cab, Seen from the Back, 1877-1878
Black pencil and blue ink wash
4⅜" × 3¼" (11.2 × 8.3 cm)
Bibliothèque Nationale, Paris

In 1882, Manet was able to paint portraits only, some in oil, some in pastel. He painted *Méry Laurent* several times, now carrying her pug-dog in her arms, now with her face shadowed by a fine veil, sometimes wearing a vast hat, sometimes a fur toque. He also painted a portrait of *René Mazeroy*, and one of *Elisa*, Méry Laurent's maid. To the Salon he sent the *Bar at the Folies-Bergère*. His usual detractors, Huysmans at their head, fired off their usual sarcasm.

By now, he could hardly walk. He was barely able to take a few steps in the garden of the house at Rueil which he occupied that summer, and thus find space enough to judge the effect of the

RUE MOSNIER WITH PAVERS, 1878
Oil on canvas, 25³⁄₁₆″ × 31½″ (64 × 80 cm)
Fitzwilliam Museum, Cambridge, Great Britain
Anonymous loan

THE HOUSE AT RUEIL, 1882
Oil on canvas, 30¹¹⁄₁₆″ × 36¼ ″ (78 × 92 cm)
Nationalgalerie Staatliche Museen
Preussicher Kulturbesitz, Berlin

IN THE CONSERVATORY. 1879
Oil on canvas, 45¼″ × 59¹⁄₁₆″ (115 × 150 cm)
Nationalgalerie Staatliche Museen
Preussicher Kulturbesitz, Berlin

THE PLUM, 1878.   Oil on canvas, 29″ × 19¾″ (73.6 × 50.2 cm)
National Gallery of Art, Washington, D.C. Collection of Mr. and Mrs. Paul Mellon

exquisite landscapes he was painting, which showed the villa amidst its trees. Soon, even these few yards became impossible. However, he continued to paint still lifes, fruits, and flowers. His friends, to whom he wrote cheerful letters, with illustrations in watercolor, came out to see him. Too weak to use a brush all the time, he more and more often made use of a medium which had long been dear to him — pastel. Thus it was that so many young Parisiennes came to pay him court, drawn by sympathy as well as a little snobbery. He found constantly, among these fresh and elegant visitors, new subjects for his pastels, carried out in a single sitting, rich in verve but also, if one may say so, of accident. They do not form, though some people have advanced the claim, the cream of his *œuvre*.

When he returned, that autumn, to the studio at 77 Rue d'Amsterdam, he still had the courage to plan a big picture, the *Bugle* (see page 88). He began the sketch on a canvas one yard high by thirty-five inches wide. His friend, the painter Henri Dupray, was the model. He owned a bugler's uniform, and a bugle. Manet made a start. The picture was destined, as he saw it, to be his submission to the Salon of 1883. But his illness had such a grip that he could not continue. What had been taken for rheumatism was, in fact, the failure of an overstressed nervous system, locomotor ataxia. Manet could bear his illness and his physical weakness no longer. At all costs he wished to be free from it. He was bed-ridden. Gangrene appeared in his left foot. An amputation was agreed to. On April 30, 1883, at 7 in the evening, Manet died. Thus departed, at the age of only fifty-one, a man whom the vast majority of his contemporaries saw as a careless amateur, a kind of bad joke; whose *œuvre*, nevertheless, added up to 420 pictures in oil, 85 pastels, 114 watercolors and numerous engravings. To each of this techniques he had brought something crisp and new. Through a kind of divination which was entirely his own, he had created a visual language ready for the generations and for the developments which were to come after him.

Manet, on his own avowal, loved society, "the perfumed, luminous delicacy of *soirées*". He liked feminine company, especially when, by virtue of wit and beauty (if not virtue itself), it was worthy of the Paris which then, through its theaters, cafés, and even its scandals, was something unique upon earth.

He was never happy away from Paris. A columnist, who signed himself Triolet, gives us a picture, in an article in the "Gaulois" in May 1881, of Manet at the age of forty-nine: "With his head and his hat thrust back, looking upward and then more with the nose than with the eyes, the eyes themselves warmed by the fire of an unbreakable will; the mouth mocking, skeptical, the blonde beard fan-shaped; with yellow gloves, a crisp cravat, superb shoes, light-colored trousers, and a flower in his buttonhole; he

77

is to be met striding along the Boulevard des Italiens with the hurried pace of a man who has a rendezvous with a pretty woman; or one sees him, at ease, smoking a good cigar, on the terrace of the Café Riche or the Café Tortoni." This dandyism, and this feigned insouciance, disguised an uneasy and vulnerable nature. At bottom, he was dominated by one passion: painting; one certitude: the worth of his own talent; and one desire: to force Paris to recognize the existence of this talent, which both the majority of the critics and the greater part of the public denied. He suffered cruelly. No one has ever desired official recognition more ardently. However he never dreamt of making the least concession to either the critics or the public.

All those who surrounded him fell under the influence of his charm, and all through his short life feminine grace meant a lot to him. Yet everything leads us to think that he was far from living loosely. The charming women he drew to him by his own natural elegance of speech and mind were to him simply agreeable models. In his letters, and in the recollections of his friends there is nothing which hints at more than courteously affectionate realtionships, nearly all of them subjected to the demands of his profession as an artist. Perhaps, sometimes, there is the faintest breath of emotions which go beyond this. He was the attentive husband of an equally devoted wife. And, among the women who sat for him, all classes of society were represented. Many belonged to the middle-class from which he himself had sprung: Marguerite de Conflans (later Madame d'Angély), Jeanne Martin, Mme Jules Guillemet, who was one of the great milliners of the time, and her sister Marguerite. Some were titled, sometimes rather oddly, like the Countess Albazzi of whom he made a curious pastel. There were also actresses: Hélène André (who became Mme Henri Dumont), Marie Colombier, whose disagreements with Sarah Bernhardt created a great stir, Rosita Mauri, who made her debut at the Opéra in 1878 in the ballet "Polyeucte". Then there is the charmingly whimsical Nina de Callias, from the upper reaches of literary and artistic bohemia; several professional models, such as Alice Lecouvé, and another Marguerite who sat for some nudes; and some young women who posed from kindness and good nature, such as Melle Saguez, in riding costume, who was the daughter of a bookseller in the Rue de Moscou, and the beautiful and charming Suzon, barmaid at the Folies-Bergère. Finally there were some of the fashionable demimondaines, who owed their celebrity both to their success in theater and the magnificence of their protectors: Henriette Hauser, the mistress of the Prince of Orange, was the model for Manet's picture *Nana* rejected by the Salon of 1877; Léontine Massin, who acted at the Vaudeville and was introduced to Manet in 1881 by her friend, M. Bernadrey; Jeanne de Marsy, who posed for *Spring* in 1881; Irma Brunner (see page 79) called "the Viennese"; the singer Emilie Ambre; Mme Valtesse de la Bigne ... and many others. Two among them, Méry Laurent and

THE VIENNESE (PORTRAIT OF IRMA BRUNNER), ca 1880. Pastel on cardboard, 25⅝″ × 18⅛″ (55 × 46 cm)
Musée d'Orsay, Paris

Emilie Ambre, showed him a delicate attentiveness and fidelity which helped him bear his illness during the last two years of his life. But among all these, Victorine Meurent occupies a quite special place from the point of view of Manet's work. Manet met her by chance in 1862. A child of bohemia, she was twenty when she began sitting for him. Until 1874 she was, with interruptions, an ideal subject: her body was not thin, but it had a nervousness and a sharpness of contour which made her the embodiment of the "modern woman" — yet without vulgarity, for Manet never confused realism and grossness. Later she herself began to paint. But the girl who had been the *Street Singer*, the bather in the *Picnic*, and *Olympia*, was to slide from misfortune to misfortune, and would meet the saddest of ends.

The Railroad, ca 1873. Woodcut by Prunaire. Bibliothèque Nationale, Paris

The Parisienne (second plate).   Woodcut by Prunaire

Another personality, one who perhaps held the warmest place of all in Manet's affections, was Berthe Morisot.   In 1860, Berthe Morisot who, accompanied by her mother and her sister Edna, was making copies in the Louvre, met Manet for the first time.   The relationship between the Manets and the Morisots became gradually closer.   They were intimate by the time, in 1868, when Berthe (who, herself a painter of delightful talent, had then exhibited her work in the Salon for three years), came, accompanied by her mother, to Manet's studio to pose for *The Balcony* (see page 37).

She was then twenty-eight years old.   A deep friendship developed between Berthe Morisot and Manet, nurtured by their mutual passion for painting.   He made many portraits of her, in oils and pastel.   Her finely chiselled features and her grave dark gaze never ceased to inspire him. On December 12, 1874, she married Manet's brother, Eugène.

Eva Gonzalès was the only artist who studied with Manet.   She admired him passionately and she died shortly after he did, in 1883.   Born in 1849, she was the daughter of the novelist Emmanuel Gonzalès.   She was a talented artist and a beautiful

A BAR AT THE FOLIES-BERGÈRE, 1881-1882
Oil on canvas, 37¾″ × 51³⁄₁₆″ (96 × 130 cm)
Courtauld Institute Galleries, London

dark-haired woman with almond-shaped eyes. In 1870 she showed several works at the Salon, including *Soldier's Son*. At the same Salon was Manet's entry, *Portrait of Eva Gonzalès*. While in Paris during the siege of 1871, Manet wrote her letters so gently affectionate as to appear almost tender — if one did not know Manet's penchant for flirtatious wit: "A 'besieged' friend asked me recently how I fared in your absence, since my admiration and friendship for you are public knowledge. ... Among all the deprivations caused by this siege, I shall certainly rank first the fact that I cannot see you anymore." For a time Berthe Morisot was jealous of this friendship. She wrote to her sister Edna, "Manet keeps lecturing me and urging me to take this Melle Gonzalès as a model. In the meantime he is starting over her portrait for the twenty-fifth time."

Lastly, among those who seem to have captivated Manet at one time or another, we must mention Isabelle Lemonnier. She was the sister-in-law of Georges Charpentier, the publisher, and related to a great jeweller on the Boulevard des Italiens. Some of the letters which Manet wrote to her seem to give a glimpse of something rather more than the relationship between a painter and a sitter whom he painted several times: "This is a hurried greeting. I should like to get one every morning, when post comes. Decidedly you don't spoil me. Either you are very busy — or very cruel."

Woman Holding a Child on Her Lap
Black wash and lead pencil
Private collection

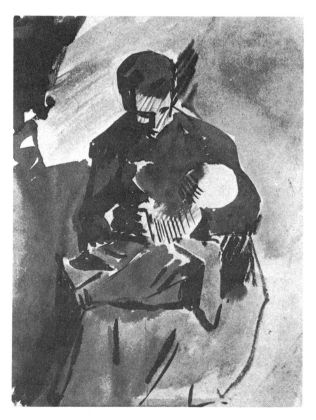

Less than a year after Manet's death, an incomplete exhibition of his work was held at the Ecole des Beaux-Arts. Zola wrote the preface to the catalogue. As always happens, many of those who had attacked him most fiercely had the gall to come there and pose as early supporters of his work. Manet had won; but the storm which he had raised had some devastating effects. The Establishment remained sulky and disconcerted in the face of an achievement which owed nothing to them, and which had triumphed whitout their aid — in fact, in spite of them. Artistic appreciation had grown outside the established art institutions, and this was a precious gain for artists.

GEORGES CLÉMENCEAU, 1879-1880.   Oil on canvas, 45⅝″ × 34¾″ (115.9 × 88.2 cm)
Kimbell Art Museum, Fort Worth, Texas

CARNATIONS AND CLEMATIS
IN A CRYSTAL VASE, ca 1882
Oil on canvas
22″ × 13¹⁵⁄₁₆″ (56 × 35.5 cm)
Musée d'Orsay, Paris

▷

LILACS IN A VASE, ca 1882
Oil on canvas
21¼″ × 16½″ (54 × 42 cm)
Nationalgalerie Staatliche
Museen
Preussicher Kulturbesitz, Berlin

THE BUGLE, 1882.   Oil on canvas, 39″ × 31⅝″ (99 × 80.3 cm)
Private collection, Switzerland

BIOGRAPHY

1832 Born on January 23, at 5 Rue des Petits-Augustins in Paris, the eldest son of an affluent high official in the Ministry of Justice.

1883 His brother Eugène was born on November 21.

1835 His brother Gustave was born on March 16.

1838-1848 A student at the Institut Poiloup in Vaugirard (what is now the fifteenth *arrondissement* of Paris).

1844-1848 Enrolled at the Collège Rollin, where he met Antonin Proust, with whom he often visited the Louvre. His maternal uncle encouraged him to draw.

1848 His father opposed his wish to become a painter. At his father's suggestion, Manet unsuccessfully tried the entrance examination for the Navy. On December 9, he sailed for Rio de Janeiro as pilot's apprentice on the vessel *Havre et Guadeloupe*, where he met Pontillon. He drew caricatures of the crew, the officers, and his shipmates.

1849 Failed again the entrance examination for the Navy. His family finally agreed to let him pursue an artistic career. He met Suzanne Leenhoff.

1850-1856 Enrolled as a student in the studio of Thomas Couture, a successful academic painter who, despite numerous quarrels, taught Manet to admire the great colorists of the past and to emphasize textures and contrasts of light and dark. Manet also set himself to study live models at the Académie Suisse and landscapes at Fontainebleau.

1852 On January 29, birth of Léon-Edouard Koëlla, known as Leenhoff, the illegitimate son of Manet and Suzanne Leenhoff. First copies of paintings at the Louvre. Trip to the Netherlands.

1853 Visit to Kassel, Dresden, Prague, Vienna, and Munich. He did studies from nature during a walking tour with Couture in Normandy. Visit to Italy: Venice, Florence, and Rome.

1855 Visited Eugène Delacroix in his studio and asked for his permission to copy *The Bark of Dante*.

1856 Left Couture's studio in February. He rented a studio on the Rue Lavoisier with Albert de Balleroy, an animal painter.

1857 Met Henri Fantin-Latour at the Louvre. He made many copies at the Louvre, especially of paintings by Velázquez, Titian, and Rubens. Journey to Italy where he copied frescoes by Andrea del Sarto.

1859 *The Absinthe Drinker* was rejected by the Salon, despite Delacroix's favorable opinion. The boy who had modelled for *The Boy with Cherries* committed suicide in Manet's studio, causing Manet to leave the studio. He moved to Rue de la Victoire. He met Degas at the Louvre.

1860 Established his studio at the Rue de Douai and settled with Suzanne Leenhoff and Léon in an apartment on the Rue de l'Hôtel de Ville in the Batignolles.

1861-1870 Established his studio at 81 Rue Guyot.

1861 *The Artist's Parents* and *The Spanish Singer* at the Salon. The painters Fantin-Latour, Alphonse Legros, Emile-Auguste Carolus-Duran, Félix Bracquemond and the writers Baudelaire, Champfleury, and Edmond Duranty came to Manet's studio to express their admiration for *The Spanish Singer*. *Reading* and *Boy with Cherries* which were exhibited at the Galerie Martinet, 26 Boulevard des Italiens. *The Surprised Nymph* is shown at the Imperial Academy in Saint Petersburg.

1862 Founding of the Société des Aquafortistes, to promote the revival of etching. Manet was a founding member, together with Bracquemond, Fantin-Latour, Johan Barthold Jongkind, Théodule Ribot, and Legros. He did *plein-air* studies in the Tuileries gardens and was a habitué of the Café Tortoni. Several etchings were published. His father died on September 25. He met Victorine Meurent, a professional model, who, for several years, was to be Manet's favorite model.

1863 Exhibition at the Galerie Martinet in March, with fourteen paintings (including *Music in the Tuileries*) and at least one etching. Opening of the "Salon des Refusés" in May, where Manet showed several paintings and etchings, and where his *Picnic* caused a scandal. Whistler introduced him to the poet Swinburne. In August he attended Delacroix's funeral with Baudelaire. He married Suzanne Leenhoff on October 28.

1864 Manet sat for the *Homage to Delacroix*, which Fantin-Latour was to submit to the Salon. He exhibited two paintings at the Salon as well as *The Battle of the Kearsarge and the Alabama* at the Galerie Cadart, 79 Boulevard des Batignolles in Paris. The Goncourt brothers visited his studio.

1865 Destroyed several of his works. Exhibited two paintings at the Galerie Martinet. He became literary agent for Baudelaire, who was in exile in Brussels. He sat for Fantin-Latour's *The Toast: Homage to Truth*. He exhibited two paintings at the Salon (*Olympia*) and several works at the Galerie Cadart. *Olympia* caused a scandal. His paintings were rejected from an exhibition at the Royal Academy in London. He made a short trip to Spain where he could study at first hand the works of Velázquez and Goya. The latter was to influence him both in technique and in style of composition. However, after this visit to Spain, he showed less interest in Spanish subject matters.

1866 Rejected by the Salon (*The Fifer*). Zola defended Manet in his review of the Salon, which caused him to resign from the newspaper "L'Evénement." In May, Manet met Monet, with whose work his own was often confused. He exhibited in Bordeaux in May and June (*Reading*). In September the Café Guerbois became the favorite meeting place for Manet and his friends. The Manet family moved to 49 Rue Saint-Pétersbourg.

1867 Held a private exhibition of fifty works at the Paris World's Fair, in a building erected at his own expense near the one Courbet had built. This show gave him a position of widespread influence as the master of the avant-garde movement. The Emperor Maximilian was executed on June 19, inspiring Manet for a series of paintings. Visit to Trouville in August. He attended the funeral of Baudelaire on September 2, in Paris.

1868 Exhibited at the Salon (*Portrait of Emile Zola* and *Woman with Parrot*). Summer in Boulogne-sur-Mer, on the Channel, followed by a brief trip to London, where Manet hoped to exhibit. He exhibited *The Dead Man* at the Havre. He met Berthe Morisot at the Louvre, and she was soon to sit for *The Balcony*. Publication of several lithographs. Two paintings shown at the Société Artistique des Bouches-du-Rhône in Marseilles.

1869 The painting *The Execution of the Emperor Maximilian* was rejected by the Salon and the publication of his print on the same subject was banned. He met Eva Gonzalès, who became his model. He exhibited two paintings (*The Balcony* and *The Luncheon*) and five etchings at the Salon. Summer in Boulogne-sur-Mer.

1870 Duel with Edmond Duranty, where Duranty was wounded. He joined a committee to change the methods for selecting a Salon jury. Jean-François Millet was the only painter on the list proposed by the committee to be elected on the jury. Manet was asked to sit for Frédéric Bazille. Two paintings at the Salon. Summer with Giuseppe de Nittis at Saint-Germain-en-Laye (*In the Garden*). Because of the Franco-Prussian war, he sent his family to Oloron-Sainte-Marie, south of Bordeaux. In November he enlisted in the National Guard, as did Degas.

1871 In February he left Paris to join his family at Oloron. On April 17, he was elected *in absentia* to a Federation of Artists to the Paris Commune. The insurrection in Paris made it impossible for him to return to Paris. He was back in Paris only after the "bloody week" of May 21-28. He spent the month of August with his family in Boulogne.

1872 Sold twenty-four paintings to Durand-Ruel. Exhibited at the Salon (*The Battle of the Kearsarge and the Alabama*). The Café "La Nouvelle Athènes" on the Place Pigalle became the favorite meeting place for Manet and his friends. Visit to the Netherlands, especially to the Frans Hals Museum in Haarlem and the Rijksmuseum in Amsterdam.

1873 Exhibited at the Salon (*Le Bon Bock* and *Repose: Portrait of Berthe Morisot*). Summer at Etaples, near Berck-sur-Mer on the Channel. In September, he met Stéphane Mallarmé in Paris. He sold five paintings to the baritone and collector Jean-Baptiste Faure.

1874 *The Railroad* was accepted at the Salon, But *The Ball at the Opera* was rejected, prompting Mallarmé to publish an article on the Salon and Manet. Opening, on May 15, of the first Impressionist exhibition at Nadar's studio, to which Manet refused to participate. Summer in Gennevilliers, near Argenteuil, where Monet lived. Following Monet's example, Manet began to paint more out-of-doors and to lighten his palette. Visit from Renoir. Marriage of Eugène Manet and Berthe Morisot on December 22. Publication of eight etchings.

1875 Illustrated Mallarmé's French translation of "The Raven" by Edgar Poe. Exhibited at the Salon (*Argenteuil*). Visit to Venice with his wife and James Tissot.

1876 Publication of Mallarmé's "L'Après-midi d'un faune" with wood engravings by Manet. He was rejected by the Salon. Manet organized an exhibition of his rejected works in his studio. He met Méry Laurent.

1877 One painting was accepted by the Salon but *Nana* was rejected.

1879 Marriage of Henri Guérard and Eva Gonzalès. Manet exhibited at the Salon (*Boating* and *In the Conservatory*). He met the singer Emilie Ambre.

1880 Exhibition of the *Execution of the Emperor Maximilian* in New York and in Boston organized by Emilie Ambre. Early symptoms of a serious illness. Exhibition organized by Georges Charpentier at the Galerie de la Vie Moderne. Manet exhibited at the Salon (*Portrait of Antonin Proust* and *At Père Lathuille's*). For reasons of ill-health, he must spend time in the country, and he settled in Bellevue, near Meudon, outside of Paris.

1881 Exhibited at the Salon (*Portrait of M. Pertuiset* and *Portrait of M. Henri Rochefort*). He spent the summer in Versailles. In November, Antonin Proust was appointed Minister for the Fine Arts and shortly after Manet was awarded the Legion of Honor.

1882 Exhibited at the Salon (*A Bar at the Folies-Bergère*). Because of his health he could not paint out-of-doors. He worked in his room on still lifes and portraits, and often preferred pastel as a medium. Summer in Rueil.

1883 Exhibited *Corner in a Café-Concert* at the Salon des Beaux-Arts in Lyons. His leg was amputated on April 20. He died on April 30 and he was buried on May 3 at the Passy Cemetery in Paris.

1884 Large retrospective of Manet's work shown at the Ecole Nationale des Beaux-Arts in Paris, thanks to the intercession of Antonin Proust and Jules Ferry, then Minister for Education and the Fine Arts.

SELECTED BIBLIOGRAPHY

CATALOGUES RAISONNÉS

GUÉRIN, Marcel. *L'Œuvre gravé de Manet*. Paris, 1944.

HARRIS, Jean Collins. *Edouard Manet. Graphic Works. A Definitive Catalogue Raisonné*. New York: Collectors' Editions, 1970.

ROUART, Denis. *Edouard Manet. Catalogue raisonné de l'œuvre peint*. Lausanne, 1975.

LETTERS OF MANET

Lettres de jeunesse 1848-1849. Voyage à Rio. Paris: L. Rouart & Fils, 1928.

Une Correspondance inédite d'Edouard Manet: Les Lettres du siège de Paris (1870-1871). Ed. by Adolphe Tabarant. Paris, 1935.

Letters with Aquarelles. New York: Pantheon, 1944.

BOOKS

ALAZARD, J. *Manet*. Lausanne, 1948.

Album de l'Autographe au Salon de 1865 et dans les ateliers. 104 pages of original sketches; 430 drawings by 352 artists. Paris, 1865.

L'Art moderne et quelques aspects de l'art ancien. With 40 poems by Henri de Régnier and many critical essays. Paris: Bernheim-Jeune.

ASTRUC, Z. *Le Salon*. Daily column published every evening during the two months long exhibition. Paris: Cadart, 1863.

BALLU. R. *Le Salon de 1878. Peintres et sculpteurs*. Paris: Quantin, 1878.

BALLU, R. *La Peinture au Salon de 1880 - Les Peintres émus, les peintres habiles*. Paris, 1880.

BASHKIRTSEFF, M. *Journal*. Paris : Charpentier, 2 vol., 1887.

BATAILLE, Georges. *Manet*. Geneva: Skira, 1955, 1983. Tr. by Austryn Wainhouse and James Emmons. New York: Skira, 1955.

BAZIN, Germain. *Edouard Manet*. Milan: Fratelli Fabbri, 1972. Paris: Diffusion Princesse, 1974.

BAZIRE, Edmond. *Manet*. With illustration after original works by Manet and engravings by Guérard. Paris: Quantin, 1884.

BEX, M. *Manet*. Paris: Tisné, 1948.

BIEZ, Jacques de. *Manet*. Lecture given on January 22, 1884, at the Salle des Capucines. Portrait after Fantin-Latour. Paris: Bachets, 1884.

BLANCHE, Jacques-Emile. *Propos de peintres - De David à Degas*. First series, with a preface by Marcel Proust. Paris, 1919.

BLANCHE, Jacques-Emile. *Manet*. With 40 plates *hors-texte*. Paris: Rieder, 1924. Tr. F.C. de Sumichrast. London, 1925.

BÜRGER, W. (Théophile Thoré). *Salons de W. Bürger, de 1861 à 1868*. 2 vol. Paris, 1870.

BURTY, Philippe. *Les Maîtres et les petits maîtres*. Paris, 1880.

CASSOU, Jean. *Manet*. Paris, 1954.

CASTAGNARY, Jules. *Les Artistes au XIXème siècle - Salon de 1861*. First series. Paris: Librairie nouvelle, 1861.

CASTAGNARY, Jules. *Salon de 1868*. Paris, 1868.

CASTAGNARY, Jules. *Le Bilan de l'année 1868*. Paris: Le Chevalier, 1869.

CASTAGNARY, Jules. *Salon (1857-1879)*. With a preface by Eugène Spulles. Paris: Charpentier, 1892.

Catalogue des tableaux de M. Edouard Manet exposés avenue de l'Alma en 1867. Paris: Imprimerie Poupart-Davyl, 30 rue du Bac.

Catalogue le l'exposition des œuvres d'Edouard Manet à l'Ecole des Beaux-Arts. With a preface by Emile Zola. Paris: Quantin, 1884.

Catalogue, vente Manet. Paintings, pastels, sketches, drawings, engravings by Manet sold after his death as the Manet Estate, at the Hôtel Drouot, February 4 and 5, 1884. Paris: Pillet & Dumoulin, 1884.

CHAMPA, Kermit. *Studies in Early Impressionism*. New Haven: Yale University Press, 1973.

CHAUMELIN, M. *L'Art contemporain*. With an introduction by W. Bürger. Paris, 1870.

CLARETIE, J. *Peintres et sculpteurs contemporains*. Paris: Charpentier & Cie, 1873.

CLARETIE, J. *L'Art et les artistes contemporains*. With a foreword on the Salon of 1876. Paris: Charpentier & Cie, 1876.

COGNIAT, Raymond. *Manet*. Paris, 1953.

COGNIAT, Raymond. *Edouard Manet* and HOOG, Michel. *La Thématique de Manet*. Paris: Hazan, 1982.

COLIN, Paul. *Edouard Manet*. Paris: Floury, 1932, 1937.

COOPER, Douglas. *Manet, Paintings*. London: Lindsay Drummond, 1950.

COURTHION, Pierre and CAILLER, Pierre, ed. *Manet raconté par lui-même et par ses amis.* Vésenaz, Geneva: P. Cailler, 1945. Tr. as *Portrait of Manet by Himself and His Contemporaries.* London, 1960.

COURTHION, Pierre. *Manet.* Paris, 1961. New York: Milton S. Fox, 1962.

DAIX, Pierre. *La Vie de peintre d'Edouard Manet.* Paris: Fayard, 1983.

DAULTE, François. *Les Dessins français de Manet à Cézanne.* Paris, 1955.

DESNOYERS, Fernand. *La Peinture de 1863 (Le Salon des Refusés).* Paris, 1863.

DORIVAL, Bernard. *Japon et Occident: Deux siècles d'échanges artistiques.* Paris, 1977.

DU CAMP, M. *Le Salon de 1861.* Paris: Bourdilliat, 1861.

DU CAMP, M. *Le Salon de 1864.* Paris: J. Claye, 1864.

DU CAMP, M. *Les Beaux-Arts à l'Exposition universelle et aux Salons de 1863, 1864, 1865, 1866, 1867.* Paris: Vve Renouard, 1867.

DUFWA, Jacques. *Winds from the East: a Study in the Art of Manet, Degas, Monet, Whistles. 1856-1886.* Stockholm: Almquist & Wiskell; Atlantic Highlands, N.J.: Humanities Press, 1981.

DUMONT, H. *Manet,* Paris, 1949.

DURANTY, Edmond. *La nouvelle peinture.* About the artists showing at the Durand-Ruel Galleires. Paris: Dentu, 1876. Ed. Marcel Guérin, Paris, 1946.

DURANTY, Edmond. *Le Pays des arts.* Paris: Charpentier, 1881.

DURET, Théodore. *Critique d'avant-garde.* Paris: Charpentier, 1885.

DURET, Théodore. *Les Peintres français en 1867.* Paris: Dentu, 1868.

DURET, Théodore. *Histoire d'Edouard Manet et de son œuvre.* With a catalogue of oils and pastels. First ed., Paris: Floury, 1902. Second and third ed., Paris: Charpentier & Fasquelle, 1906, 1919. Fourth ed., Paris: Bernheim-Jeune, 1926. Tr. by E. Waldmann, Berlin, 1910.

DURET, Théodore. *Manet and the French Impressionists.* Tr. by J.E. Crawford Flitch. London: Richards, 1910. Philadelphia: Lippincott, 1912.

EKLUND, H. *Edouard Manet.* Stockholm: Forum, 1950.

ETIENNE, L. *Le Jury et les exposants - Le Salon des Refusés.* Paris, 1863.

EVANS, T.W. *Le Second Empire.* Memoirs tr. by I. Philippi. Paris: Plon, 1928.

FARWELL, Beatrice. *Manet and the Nude: A Study of Iconography in the Second Empire.* Doctoral dissertation University of California, Los Angeles, 1971. New York, London: Garland, 1981.

FELS, Florent. *Edouard Manet.* Paris: Librairie de France, 1928.

FÉNÉON, Felix. *L'Impressionnisme en 1886.* Paris: La Vogue, 1886.

FLAMENT, A. *La Vie de Manet.* Paris: Plon et Nourrit, 1928.

FLESCHER, Sharon. *Zacharie Astruc: Critic, Artist and Japonist.* Doctoral dissertation, Columbia University, 1977. New York, 1978.

FLORISOONE, Michel. *Manet.* Monaco: Les Documents d'art, 1947.

FOURCAUD, L. de. *L'Evolution de la peinture en France au XIXème siècle.* Paris, 1890.

FOURNEL, François Victor. *Les Artistes français contemporains: Peintres, sculpteurs.* Tours, 1884.

GAUTIER, Théophile. *Abécédaire du Salon de 1861.* Paris: Dentu, 1861.

GAY, Peter. *Art and Act, On Causes in History, Manet, Gropius, and Mondrian.* New York: Harper & Row, 1976.

GEFFROY, Gustave. *Edouard Manet.* Paris: Dentu, 1894.

GIMPEL, René. *Journal d'un collectionneur marchand de tableaux.* Paris, 1963. Tr. by J. Rosenberg, *Diary of an Art Dealer.* New York, 1966.

GLASER, Curt. *Edouard Manet - Faksimiles nach Zeichnungen und Aquarellen mit einer Vorrede.* Munich: Piper, 1922.

GONSE, Louis, ed. *Les Beaux-Arts et les Arts décoratifs à l'Exposition de 1878.* Paris, 1878.

GOSELIN, T. *Histoire anecdotique des salons de peinture depuis 1873.* Paris, 1881.

GRABER, Hans. *Edouard Manet nach eigenen und fremden Zeugnissen.* Basel: Schwabe, 1941.

GRAMANTIERI, T. *Il caso Manet.* Rome: Palombi, 1944.

HAMILTON, George Heard. *Manet and His Critics.* New Haven, Conn., London: Yale University Press, 1954.

HANSON, Anne Coffin. *Manet and the Modern Tradition.* New Haven, Conn., London: Yale University Press, 1977.

HOFMANN, Werner. *Nana: Mythos und Wirklichkeit.* Cologne, 1973.

HOPP, Gisela. *Untersuchung zur Bildgestaltung bei Edouard Manet. Rang und Aufgaben der Farbe.* Doctoral dissertation, Hamburg, 1966. Published as: *Edouard Manet. Farbe und Bildgestalt.* Berlin: de Gruyter, 1968.

HOUSSAYE, H. *L'Art français depuis dix ans.* Paris, 1883.

HUYSMANS, J.K. *L'Art moderne.* Paris: Charpentier, 1883.

ISAACSON, Joel. *Manet: Le Déjeuner sur l'herbe.* New York, 1972.

JAMOT, Paul et WILDENSTEIN, Georges. *Manet, catalogue critique.* Paris: Les Beaux-Arts, 1932.

JEDLICKA, Gotthard. *Edouard Manet.* Erlenbach, Zurich: Rentsch, 1941.

LEFENESTRE, G. *L'Art vivant. La peinture et la sculpture aux Salons de 1868 à 1877.* Paris, 1881.

LARAN, Jean and LE BAS, Georges. *Edouard Manet.* With an int. by L. Hourticq and 48 plates *hors-texte.* Paris: Librairie centrale des Beaux-Arts, 1911. Philadelphia: Lippincott, 1912. London: Heinemann, 1912.

LECOMTE, G. *L'Art impressionniste.* Paris, 1892.

LÉGER, C. *Manet.* Paris: Crès, 1931.

LEIRIS, Alain de. *The Drawings of Edouard Manet.* Berkeley: University of California Press, 1969.

LEIRIS, Alain de. *Le Ruban au cou d'Olympia.* Paris, 1981.

LEYMARIE, Jean. *Manet et les impressionnistes au Musée du Louvre.* Paris, 1948.

LEYMARIE, Jean. *Manet.* Paris: Hazan, 1951.

MARCEL, H. *La Peinture française au XIXème siècle.* Paris, 1905.

MARTIN, Kurt. *Edouard Manet: Die Erschiessung Kaiser Maximilians von Mexiko.* Berlin: Gebr. Marrn, 1948.

MARTIN, Kurt. *Edouard Manet, Aquarelle, Pastelle.* Basel: Phoebus Verlag, 1955. Tr. as *Edouard Manet, Watercolours and Pastels* London: Faber & Faber, 1959.

MATHEY, François. *Olympia: Manet.* Paris: Vendôme, 1948.

MATHEY, François. *Edouard Manet, Peintures.* Paris, 1949.

MATHEY, François. *Manet. Peintures réapparues.* Paris, 1963.

MATHEY, François. *Manet, Dessins et peintures réapparues.* Paris, 1966.

MAUCLAIR, Camille. *L'Impressionnisme, son histoire, son esthétique, ses maîtres.* Paris, 1904.

MAUCLAIR, Camille. *Les Etats de la peinture française de 1850 à 1920.* Paris: Payot, 1921.

MAUNER, George L. *Manet, peintre-philosophe. A Study of the Painter's Themes.* University Park: Pennsylvania State University Press, 1975.

MEIER-GRAEFE, Julius. *Manet und sein Kreis.* Berlin, 1902.

MEIER-GRAEFE, Julius. *Entwicklungsgeschichte der modernen Kunst.* 3 vol., 1904.

MEIER-GRAEFE, Julius. *Impressionisten (Guys, Manet, Van Gogh, Pissarro, Cézanne).* Munich, Lepzig: Piper, 1907.

MEIER-GRAEFE, Julius and KLOSSOWSKI, E. *Collection Cheramy: Catalogue raisonné.* With studies on the most important masters of the collection. 127 heliotypes and 2 helioengravings *hors-texte.* Munich: Piper, 1908.

MEIER-GRAEFE, Julius. *Edouard Manet.* Munich: Piper, 1912.

MEIER-GRAEFE, Julius. *Edouard Manet.* Munich, 1908.

MOORE, George. *Modern Painting.* New enl. ed. London, 1898, 1912.

MOORE, George. *Confessions of a Young Man.* London, 1904.

MOORE, George. *Memoirs of My Dead Life.* London, 1906.

MOREAU-NELATON, Etienne. *Manet graveur et lithographe.* With an original etching and 125 reproductions. Paris: Delteil, 1906.

MOREAU-NELATON, Etienne. *Manet raconté par lui-même.* 2 vol. with 353 reproductions. Paris: Laurens, 1926.

MORTIMER, R. *Edouard Manet, A Bar at the Folies Bergère.* London, 1944.

NEISS, R.J. *Zola, Cézanne and Manet. A Study of l'Œuvre.* Ann Arbor: University of Michigan Press, 1968.

NITTIS, Joseph de. *Notes et souvenirs.* Paris: Librairies et Imprimeries réunies, 1895.

ORIENTI, Sandra. *Opera pittorica di Edouard Manet.* Int. by M. Venturi. Milan: Rizzoli, 1967. *The Complete Paintings of Manet.* Int. by Phoebe Pool. New York: Abrams, 1967. New York: Rizzoli, 1971. *Tout l'œuvre peint d'Edouard Manet.* Int. byr Denis Rouart. Paris: Flammarion, 1970.

PERRUCHOT, Henri. *La Vie de Manet.* Paris: Hachette, 1959, Tr. as *Edouard Manet.* New York: Barnes & Noble, 1962.

PIERARD, L. *Manet l'incompris.* Paris: Sagittaire, 1944.

PROUST, Antonin. *Edouard Manet, Souvenirs.* Expanded and revised edition of several articles. Paris: Laurens, 1913. Berlin: Cassirer, 1929.

REFF, Theodore. *Manet: Olympia.* New York: Viking, 1976.

REIFENBERG, B. *Manet.* Bern: Scherz, 1947, 1925.

REWALD, John. *Edouard Manet, Pastels.* Oxford: Cassirer, 1947.

REWALD, John. *History of Impressionism.* Rev. ed. New York: Museum of Modern Art, 1980.

REY, Robert. *Choix de 64 dessins de Manet.* Paris, New York: Braun, 1932.

REY, Robert. *Manet.* Paris: Hypérion, 1938. Tr. by E.B. Shaw. London, New York: Hyperion, 1938.

RICHARDSON, John. *Edouard Manet, Paintings and Drawings.* London: Phaidon, 1958, 1982.

ROSENTHAL, Léon. *Manet aquafortiste et lithographe.* Paris: Le Goupy, I°-25.

ROOS, Novelene. *Manet's «Bar at the Folies Bergère» and the Myth of Popular Illustration.* Doctoral dissertation, Washington University, 1980. Ann Arbor, Mich.: UMI Research Press, 1982.

SAINTE-CROIX, C. de. *Edouard Manet.* Paris: Fabre, 1909.

SANDBLAD, Nils Gösta. *Manet, Three Studies in Artistic Conception.* Lund: CWK Gleerup, 1954.

SASAKI, Hideya. *Manet.* Tokyo: Shueisha, 1970.

SAVARUS, P. de. *Dix années d'art. Souvenirs des expositions.* Paris, 1879.

SCHNEIDER, Pierre. *The World of Manet 1832-1883.* New York: Time-Life Books, 1968. *Manet et son temps.* Paris, 1972.

SEVERINI, Giorgio. *Edouard Manet.* Rome: Valori Plastici, 1924.

SHINODA, Hajime et al. *Manet.* Tokyo: Shogakukan, 1978.

STUCKLEY, Charles F. *Manet.* Mount Vernon, N.Y.: Metropolitan Museum of Art, 1983.

TABARANT, Adolphe. *Manet: Histoire catalographique.* Paris: Montaigne, 1931. This definitive work is stripped of all flourishes and it establishes the extent of Manet's work. The least incidents which played a part in the life and the work of the artist are brought together with a patience and piety that every historian must recognize. No one can write about Manet without referring to this book.

TABARANT, Adolphe. *La Vie artistique au temps de Baudelaire.* Paris, 1942. Reprint, Paris, 1963.

TABARANT, Adolphe. *Manet et ses œuvres.* Paris: Gallimard, 1947.

THIIS, J. *Manet.* Copenhagen, 1917.

TSCHUDI, Hugo von. *Edouard Manet.* Berlin: Cassirer, 1902.

VALERY, Paul. *Degas, Manet, Morisot.* Tr. by David Paul. Int. by Douglas Cooper. New York: Pantheon, 1960.

VAST-RICOUART and GROS-KOST. *Le Salon réaliste.* Cover illustration by Manet. Paris: P. Ollendorf, May 1, 1880.

VAUDOYER, J.L. *Edouard Manet.* Paris: Ed. du Dimanche, 1955.

VENTURI, Lionello. *Four Steps Toward Modern Art: Giorgione, Caravaggio, Manet, Cézanne.* New York: Columbia University Press, 1956.

WADLEY, Nicholas. *Manet.* London: Hamlyn, 1967.

WALDEMAR, Georges. *Manet et la carence du spirituel.* Paris: Quatre Chemins, 1932.

WALDMANN, E. *Edouard Manet.* Berlin: Cassirer, 1923.

WILSON, J. *Manet: dessins, aquarelles, eaux-fortes, lithographies, correspondance.* Paris: Huguette Berès, 1978.

ZOLA, Emile. *Mon Salon.* Paris: Librairie centrale, 1866.

ZOLA, EMILE. *Mes Haines.* Literary and artistic essays. Paris, 1866.

ZOLA, Emile. *Edouard Manet.* Biographical and critical study, with a portrait of Manet by Bracquemond, and an etching by Manet after *Olympia.* Paris: Dentu, 1867.

MAIN EXHIBITIONS

1966-1967 *Edouard Manet 1832-1883*, Philadelphia Museum of Art and Art Institute of Chicago.

1969 *Manet and Spain: Prints and Drawings*, Museum of Art, University of Michigan Ann Arbor.

1973 *Nana: Mythos und Wirklichkeit*, Kunsthalle, Hamburg.

1974 *Centenaire de l'Impressionnisme*, Galeries Nationales du Grand Palais, Paris and The Metropolitan Museum of Art, New York.

1974-1975 *L'Estampe impressionniste*, Bibliothèque Nationale, Paris.

1977 *The Cult of Images*, University of California, Santa Barbara.

1977 *Edouard Manet: Das Graphische Werk*, Villa Schneider, Ingelheim am Rhein.

1978 *From Manet to Toulouse-Lautrec: French Lithographs 1860-1900*, British Museum, London. *Manet*, Galerie Huguette Berès, Paris.

1981 *Edouard Manet and "The Execution of Maximilian,"* Bell Gallery, List Art Center, Brown University, Providence, R.I.

1982-1983 *Manet and Modern Paris*, National Gallery of Art, Washington, D.C.

1983 *Manet 1832-1883*, Galeries Nationales du Grand Palais, Paris and The Metropolitan Museum of Art, New York.

1984 *L'Impressionnisme dans les collections romandes.* Fondation de l'Hermitage, Lausanne.

1984-1985 *A Day in the Country: Impressionism and the French Landscape.* Los Angeles County Museum of Art; The Art Institute of Chicago; Grand Palais, Paris.

ILLUSTRATIONS

Absinthe Drinker (The) 9
After the Bath 47
Argenteuil 52
Artist's Parents (The) 12

Balcony (The) 37
Ball at the Opera 49
Bar at the Folies-Bergère (A) 82-83
Before the Mirror 66
Boat on the Beach 63
Boating 50-51
Boy with Cherries 16
Boy with a Sword 21
Bugle (The) 88

Cab (The) 72
Carnations and Clematis in a Crystal Vase ... 86
Cats' Rendezvous (The) 32
Choirboy (The) 6
Convalescent (The) 30

Dead Man (The) 20
Dead Toreador (The) 20

Execution of the Emperor Maximilian (The)   28, 29

Fifer (The) 17
Fisherman (Study of a) 60

Game of Croquet (The) 56
Georges Clémenceau 85
Grand Canal, Venice (The) 61

Harbor at Calais (The) 34
Head of a Woman 46
Horses, Carts, and Boats 62
House at Rueil (The) 74

In the Conservatory 75
In the Garden 39
Isabelle with a Bonnet 59

Lemon (The) 44
Lilacs in a Vase 87
Lola de Valence 18

Loth and His Daughters 69
Luncheon (The) 26-27

Madame Manet on a Blue Sofa 64
Mirabelle Plum (The) 58
Monet Painting in His Boat 53
M. Auguste Manet 13
Music in the Tuileries 5
Music in the Tuileries (Study for) 5

Nana 67
Nude Sitting (Study of) 46

Olympia 14-15
Olympia (Study for) 70
On the Beach 35

Parisienne (The) 81
Picnic (The) 22-23
Plum (The) 76
Portrait of Emile Zola 40
Portrait of Irma Brunner (The Viennese) 79
Portrait of the Poet Stéphane Mallarmé 65
Portrait of Victorine Meurent 11

Railroad (The) 80
Reading 41
Repose: Portrait of Berthe Morisot 38
Rue Mosnier with Pavers 73

Scene on a Beach (Study for) 71
Sketch after an Italian Fresco 7
Spanish Singer (The Guitarero) 19
Street Singer (The) 10

Three Studies of A Monk Sitting 7

Woman (Study of a) 42
Woman at Her Toilet 31
Woman at Her Toilet (Study for) 47
Woman Holding a Child on Her Lap 84
Woman with the Garter 68
Women (Studies of) 43

Young Boy 24
Young Lady in 1866 (Woman with Parrot) ... 25
Young Woman Sitting 54

We wish to thank the owners of the pictures reproduced herein, as well as the collectors who did not want to have their name mentioned. Our special thanks go to Mr. François Daulte in Lausanne for his kind and valuable assistance.

MUSEUMS

BELGIUM: Tournai, Musée des Beaux-Arts.

DANMARK: Copenhagen, Ny Carlsberg Glyptotek - Copenhagen, Ordrupgaardsamlingen, Charlottenlund.

FRANCE: Paris, Bibliothèque Nationale - Paris, Musée d'Orsay - Paris, Musée du Louvre, Cabinet des Dessins.

GERMANY: Berlin, Nationalgalerie Staatliche Museen Preussicher Kulturbesitz - Frankfurt, Städelches Kunstinstitut - Hamburg, Kunsthalle - Mannheim, Städtische Kunsthalle - Munich, Bayerische Staatsgemäldesammlungen.

PORTUGAL: Lisbon, Museu Fondaçao Calouste Gulbenkian.

UNITED KINGDON :   Cambridge, Fitzwilliam Museum - London, Courtauld Institute Galleries - London, National Gallery.

UNITED STATES OF AMERICA: Boston, Museum of Fine Arts - Fort Worth, Texas, Kimbell Art Museum - New York, Metropolitan Museum of Art - New York, Solomon R. Guggenheim Museum - Providence, Rhode Island, Museum of Art, Rhode Island School of Design - Washington, D.C., National Gallery of Art.

PROTOGRAPHS

Jörg P. Anders, Berlin - Artothek, Planegg/Munich, Germany - Bergerhausen, Mannheim - Carmelo Guadagno, New York - Ralph Kleinhempel, Hamburg - Service de Documentation Photographique de la Réunion des Musées Nationaux, Paris - Woldbye, Copenhagen.